Sales Intelligence: A Smarter Way to Sell

Copyright ©2015 by Timo T. Aijo All rights reserved.

No part of this publication may be reproduced, distributed, or transmitted in any form or by any means, electronic, mechanical, photocopying, recording, scanning, or otherwise attached to any platform of any kind, or be stored in a database or retrieval system, except as permitted under Section 107 or 108 of the 1976 United States Copyright Act, without the prior written permission of the publisher. Any and all requests to the Publisher for permission should be addressed to Permissions, Big Brown House Publishing Company, PO box 468, Ashland, MA 01721.

Limit of Liability/Disclaimer of Warranty: While both the publisher and the author have used their best efforts in preparing this book, they make no representations or warranties with respect to the accuracy or completeness of the contents of this book and specifically disclaim any implied warranties of merchantability or fitness for a particular purpose. No warranty may be created or extended by sales representatives or sales materials of any kind. The advice and strategies contained herein represent the opinions of the author, and may not be suitable for your situation, and should be reviewed as such. Always consult a professional prior to utilizing any idea, strategy, or advice. Neither the publisher nor author shall be liable for any loss or damages of any kind.

Big Brown House Publishing Company also publishes books in other than print format. Content may vary from one media to another.

This edition is published by arrangement with Timo T. Aijo.

Big Brown House Publishing Company
Po Box 468
Ashland, MA 01721
www.BigBrownHousePublishing.com

Big Brown House Publishing Company is a publishing Company offering editorial, photography, and text composition to authors.

Cover art template by NaCDS and CoverDesignStudio.com
Interior book design and editing by Deborah Aijo.

Printed in the Unites States of America

Library of Congress Cataloging-in-Publication Data:

Aijo, Timo T.
  Sales Intelligence: The Smarter Way to Sell
  Includes bibliographical references
        1.Selling 2. Business 3. Management 4. Customer 5. Marketing
        I. Aijo, Timo II. Title

ISBN 978-0-9965765-0-5

To all sales champions out there

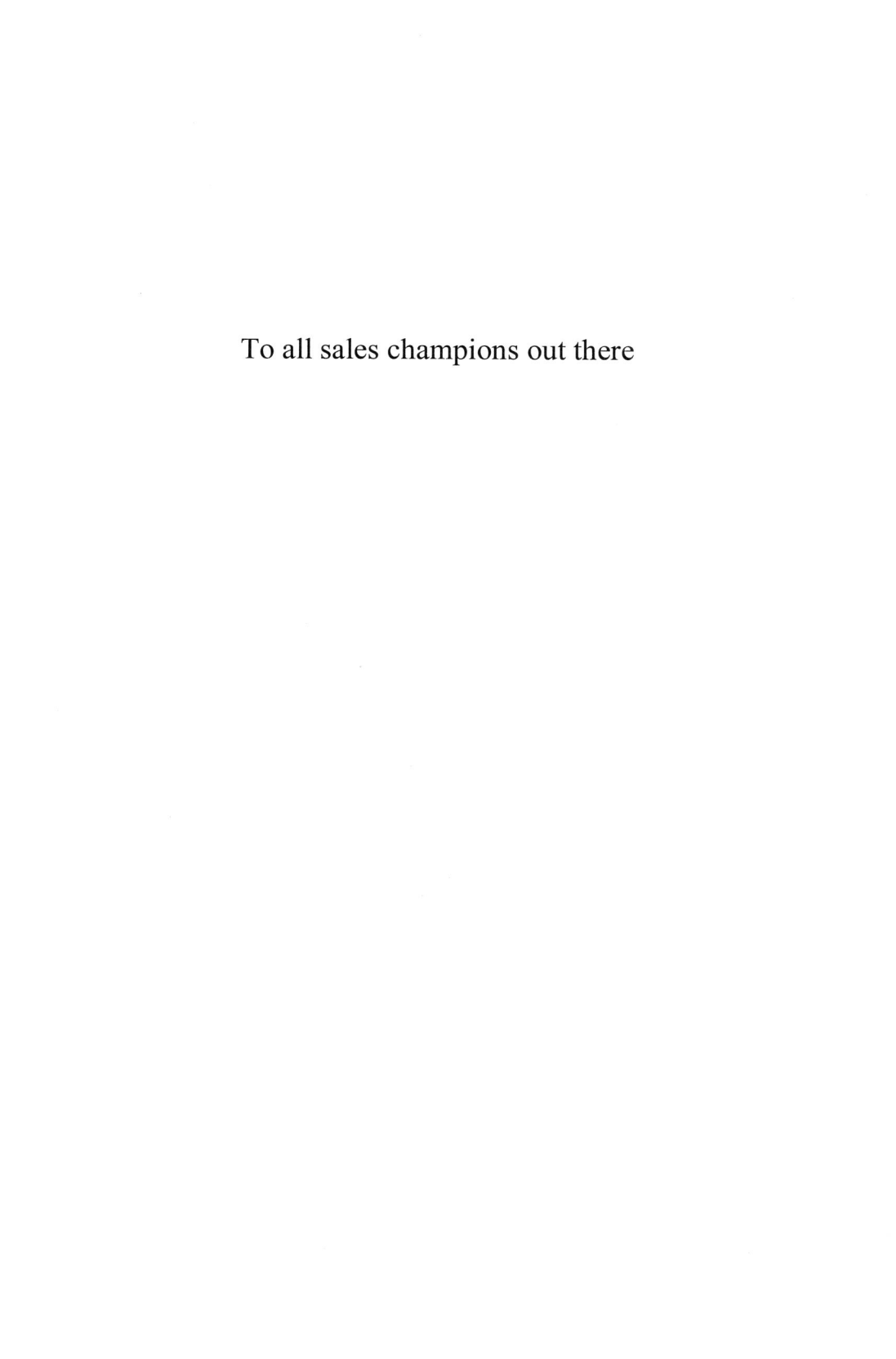

# Contents

PART I: GETTING STARTED .................................................................... 3
1. THE BASICS ............................................................................................ 5
    What is the Salesperson's Job? ................................................................ 5
    The Company ............................................................................................ 7
    Training ..................................................................................................... 19
    Your Product ............................................................................................. 24
2. SALES PROCESS: THE LADDER APPROACH ................................. 33
3. THE SALES PERSONALITY ............................................................... 41
4. A CLOSER LOOK AT COMPETITOR INFORMATION ..... 47
    Who or What Are You Competing Against? ....................... 47
    Analyzing the Competition ................................................. 48
    Competitor Sales Styles ...................................................... 50

PART II: THE SALES CALL .......................................................... 53
5. THE PRODUCTIVE SALES CALL OR MEETING .............. 55
    Preparing for the Call or Meeting ....................................... 55
    During the Call or Meeting ................................................. 58
    After the Call or Meeting .................................................... 61
    First Impressions ................................................................. 63

PART III: QUOTATIONS & PRICING .......................................... 67
6. WHAT TO OFFER AT WHAT PRICE .................................... 69
    Start With a Need to be Filled ............................................ 69
    Price Shock Theory ............................................................. 70
    Full Offer or Incremental Bidding ...................................... 72

    Options ................................................................................ 75
    Delivering Your Offer ......................................................... 76
**7. QUOTATION ANALYSIS** ................................................... 79
    What to Quote .................................................................... 80
    Setting Prices ..................................................................... 82
    Who Are the Other Bidders? ............................................... 84
    Increase Your Chances of Getting an Order ....................... 86
    Create an Evaluation System ............................................. 88
**8. PRICING AND PRICE ELASTICITY** ................................ 91
    Project Budgets ................................................................. 92
    Quoting to Stay in the Game .............................................. 92
    Discounts ........................................................................... 93
    Pricing Strategies .............................................................. 94
    Turning the Discussion to Value ........................................ 98
    Product Price Comparison ................................................. 98
    Features and Options ....................................................... 100
    Moving to an All Inclusive Price ....................................... 101
    The Sweetness of a Low Price ......................................... 102

**PART IV: TRACKING & ORGANIZATION** ........................ 105
**9. TRACKING QUOTATIONS** ............................................. 107
    The Top 5-Next 5 Concept ............................................... 108
    The Smelly Fish Quotation ............................................... 111
**10 PRIORITIZING TO MAXIMIZE TIME** ............................ 113
    Common Time Robbers ................................................... 113
    Tracking Your Work ......................................................... 117

**PART V: THE CUSTOMER** .................................................. 119

## 11. LISTEN TO THE CUSTOMER .................................................. 121
- Why Do Customers Buy From You? ................................... 121
- Why Customers Don't Buy From You ................................ 125
- Customer Motives for Buying ........................................... 126
- Team Purchasing ............................................................... 130

## 12. PENETRATING THE CUSTOMER ORGANIZATION .... 131
- Width x Depth = Sales ...................................................... 131
- The Whisperer ................................................................... 131
- Why Three Neutrals Are Better Than Two For's and One Against ............................................................................... 132
- Keeping the Customer's Trust .......................................... 134
- Decision Makers ............................................................... 135
- It's OK to Take No for an Answer ..................................... 137
- Classifying Customers ...................................................... 137

## 13. WHAT'S REALLY GOING ON? ......................................... 141
- The Brush-Off .................................................................... 141
- Ability to Squeeze a Decision ........................................... 143
- The Cold Shoulder Treatment ........................................... 145
- The Rule of Non-Negotiation ............................................ 146
- Winning an Invitation to the Final Meeting ...................... 148
- The Final Meeting ............................................................. 149

## 14. ANALYZING CUSTOMERS .............................................. 153
- Be Objective in Your Analysis .......................................... 156
- Get a Second Opinion ....................................................... 158
- Utilize Your Organization .................................................. 158
- Momentum Can Change on a Dime ................................. 159

## 15. CUSTOMER CONTACT: HOW OFTEN? ......................... 163
- One Time Customer versus the Repeat Customer .......... 165

    Weekly or Biweekly Contact ................................................. 166
    Monthly Contact ..................................................................... 168
    Quarterly or Yearly Contact .................................................. 169

PART VI: MANAGING A SALES FORCE .............................. 171
16. MEASURING AND REPORTING SALES SUCCESS: KEY PEFORMANCE INDICATORS ................................................. 173
    The Relationship With Your Manager ................................ 182
    Enthusiasm or Experience .................................................... 183
    Overall Economy as a Factor in Sales ............................... 186
17. SALES COMPENSATION ................................................. 187
18. CONTRACTS ......................................................................... 191
    Legal Aspects of Sales ......................................................... 195
    Drafting and Negotiating Contracts ................................... 196
    Unacceptable Contracts and Bad Contracts: Who Is Responsible? ........................................................................ 200
19. RULES AND ETHICS OF SELLING ............................... 207
BIBLIOGRAPHY ....................................................................... 211

# INTRODUCTION

Twenty years ago, I landed my first position in sales. Since then, I've sold multi-million dollar projects in over 20 countries, traveled with government delegations, and made plenty of mistakes. Even if at the time I thought I was doing everything right. It's easy to pick these out years after the fact, maybe partially because it's easier to admit them now, but mainly because these days I have the knowledge and the tools to analyze the situations in detail.

Over the years as I gained more sales intelligence – both in information and smarts – I realized that I was able to predict whether I would get a particular sale or not. When the light went on it was so easy, but no one else seemed to be using the same methods. It's taken hundreds of actual sales cases to accumulate the data to develop my methodology. The fact is sales is a constant state of information gathering and analysis. There are numerous pieces of data that will affect your sale – from where your company is positioned in the market, to manufacturing capacity, to a harmless tidbit of organizational information received over lunch. The more quality information you have, the better your sales results will be.

Most of this information can't be purchased from commercially available reports or found in statistical research, and a motivational kick in the bottom isn't going to help. Many authors tell you what your goal should be, but they don't tell you how to get there. Knowing that, statistically, you will win every fifth quote is great, but how does that information help you with the one you are working on now? And, every quote is decided by somebody. Who are they?

Everyone in sales is looking for that purple pill: the one that helps you sell anything to anyone. Unfortunately, it doesn't exist. Hard work, avoiding mistakes, and a strong analytical approach will win you sales.

# PART I.
# GETTING STARTED

# 1.

# THE BASICS

## What is the Salesperson's Job?

Companies do not hire salespeople and give them unlimited time to produce results. In fact, exactly the opposite is true. Your employer expects you to be productive whether you are a seasoned sales professional, been in your career for a short time, or just been hired for your first job. In the beginning, your manager may seem indifferent to results, and assures you how they want you to just learn the ropes. But regardless of how they appear, the fact is they are wondering when (and if) you will pull your own weight. Do not misinterpret the leeway they are giving you to settle in as standard operating procedure because it definitely is not.

What does productive mean to the sales professional? It means not just making phone calls and writing quotations; it means making phone calls, writing quotations, and engaging in customer interactions that turn to profitable orders for your employer.

Your job is to convince customers to order from you. This means that you, as a sales professional, have to make sure that the customer

- Understands your product's or service's features
- Believes that your product fulfills their needs better than the competitor's product
- Believes in the capability of your company to execute and follow through potential orders

- Does not get an impression that they are taken advantage of in the form of quality, price, or anything else (Customers need to know that they did well or got a good deal.)
- Thinks of you and your company first when a need arises
- Has no doubt about you, your product, or your company

**The Hard Truth**

You have competition. It doesn't always matter how good a salesperson, company, or a product is because it is rarely the only supplier offering the same product or solution. In fact, the market is flooded with more products and competitors than the customer base can support. The fight for customers is real, and it is fierce.

Since there is an abundance of products and companies for a customer to choose from, it is important to take full advantage of every possible sales situation and treat every potential customer like the most important customer of your career. It can mean the difference between success and failure; it's not always the better product or company that wins. A company must monetize their experience and good references.

Contrary to popular belief, price is not the only determining factor in a sale. There are many components that contribute to individual sales, and the only way to create a lasting relationship and history with a customer is by repeatedly executing individual sales one after another. If a customer hasn't ordered from you yet, how could there be a relationship? A base level relationship between the seller and the buyer is created during the quotation phase, but it is solidified by the success of an order when both parties are relying – and are somewhat dependent – on each other.

So, how do you gain an upper hand with the competition? You analyze available information and you learn from it. This process is a never ending cycle, and works as a good tool for quickly responding to changing market conditions or to new competitors.

## The Company

Know how your company conducts business and where it stands in the marketplace. With this information you can quickly identify target customers and make efficient use of your time.

Knowing your company means more than having an overall picture of the company. You want a complete as possible analysis to aid you with your job. Gather information from multiple sources for a well rounded view. Read documents; talk to people. It's easy to spend a few hours online searching for company related information. You may have friends or acquaintances that have worked for the company or been their customer. Any information you can piece together is useful. This may seem obvious, but most people don't do it. I promise you will be embarrassed if you get caught in a sales situation where the customer knows more about your company or product than you do. How will you portray yourself as an expert then?

Begin with general information about the company. Below are some of the questions you should ask yourself:

### Where in the Market is the Company Positioned?

Whether you are selling a product or service, you need to look at that product market as a whole. Each vertical includes the low-price leader; the high-priced, perceived-quality supplier; local suppliers; and niche players. The rest can be classified as "mass" or "me too" companies that don't really have strong differentiators. Draw a chart and position your company within that marketplace, and compare your offering to your competitors' to determine your product's strong features. This exercise should be done periodically – maybe once per year. It's good practice to complete the new charts first before comparing them to previous years.

You may have a different view of the market than you did a year ago, and you want to capture that in your new analysis before your opinion is affected by past information. If you work for a bigger company, they most likely already have this information, but if you are starting a company of your own, you absolutely need to do this for your own benefit.

## What is the Company's Size and Ability to Execute Orders?

Company size and market position provide an idea of the company's ability to deliver products or services. A good rule of thumb is that no single customer will order more than 50% of a company's yearly turnover or capacity. The reason: anything more is just too large for the company to handle.

On the flip side, if you are a business owner, you should avoid the situation where one customer generates more than one third of your revenues because it makes you too reliant on that one customer. A good plan is to have a few of the largest customers bring in a combined 50%-60% of the company's turnover.

> Company A manufactures mailboxes. They sell an average of 8,000 mailboxes per month, so about 100,000 mailboxes per year. The standard delivery time for an average order of 250 mailboxes is five weeks. We can assume that on average they get 40 (give or take) orders per month. What will happen if Company A receives a single order for 50,000 units? At current production levels, it will take over six months to fulfill that one order alone. If we assume that Company A also keeps its other customers, they are receiving orders for an additional 50,000 mailboxes during that six month period. How will they be able to fulfill all their orders?

The quick answer is to increase production, but it is difficult to increase production by 100% for a period of six months. The company will need to ramp up its entire infrastructure, including equipment and workforce, to meet the demand. It will be expensive, and after that big order has been delivered what will Company A do with the increased production capacity if there are no additional orders? They will have to dismantle the excess capacity, which will also cost money. In the end, all these additional expenses may not only cause the company to make less profit than anticipated, they could actually lose money.

A possible alternative is for the salesperson to steer the negotiations and contract toward a plan where Company A increases production by 20%-25%, and the customer allows 14-18 months to deliver the 50,000 mailboxes. This way the ramp up in production does not have to be so dramatic, and the duration of the contract gives the company time to see if the new production level can be sustained by a more permanent increased demand.

How do you explain this to an eager salesperson who is about to get that order? What if the customer is unwilling or incapable of modifying the original delivery schedule? The fact is if Company A does not accept the order, the customer will go elsewhere. There are few things as demotivating to a salesperson than having a customer ready to order, but the internal organization's inertia prevents it from happening.

Manufacturing capacity directly affects the sales process, but is an issue often overlooked by salespeople. Or, they are bluntly told, "We can't do it," instead of starting with the hypothesis that the answer to the customer must be "yes," and working on how to get there.

Yet, if manufacturing can't handle an order that large or it is too expensive to temporarily ramp up production, it is important that the sales team understands that just increasing production by 100% may not be a viable solution for a one time sale. As illustrated in the example above, economies of scale do not necessarily always work on peak growth if there are no other customers or factors supporting that peak growth. An experienced customer knows this. An experienced sales manager also knows this. As demonstrated in the example above, it may actually be more profitable for Company A to concentrate on orders for 10,000-20,000 units because growth is more manageable and profitable.

Am I telling you to not go after big orders? No, of course not. I am saying that the probability of a customer ordering from you when they know your company does not have the capacity in place to fulfill their order is very low, and you must take this into consideration when managing your time. Don't be blinded by big numbers and throw all your efforts into one impossible order only to be crushed if it falls through, or goes to a competitor after all your hard work. The reality is a customer will ask how many times your company has executed an order of this size, and an answer of "none" creates a doubt in the customer's mind. Doubt, as we discussed at the beginning of this chapter, is not a good thing. It is safer and more productive to spend a greater share of time on quotes with a high probability of turning to an order, and less time on the huge project with low probability. More about analyzing and ranking quotations in Chapter 9.

## Who are the Company's Ideal Customers?

It is imperative to identify your customer because the marketplace is flooded with products, and every supplier has their strong points. Not every prospect will be your customer. Targeting the wrong type of customer is a waste of time, and your order yield will be low. When you have a clear picture of your ideal customer and concentrate on them first, you will be more productive and your success rate will be higher.

When I say ideal customer I am not talking about the biggest customer; I am talking about the typical, existing, order-placing customer. What characteristics do most of the company's customers have in common?

# GETTING STARTED 11

Are they in the same industry? How big are they? What products do they order, and how often? Why do they buy from this company? The goal is to identify this ideal customer with a set of attributes. These attributes can then be used to see which other potential customers have them too.

You are looking for a niche demand that your company fills. Identifying the ideal customer provides you with the information necessary to create a list of criteria to qualify potential customers to see if they belong to this group or not. It also helps you pinpoint key words and lingo that will be useful in marketing to these customers.

> I would like to buy a duck call. What brand would you suggest? I probably didn't have to finish my question before you were thinking of the hugely popular show Duck Dynasty, and the company Duck Commander. Who are Duck Commander's main customers? Even if you've never been duck hunting, you can probably name some attributes of Duck Commander's customers. This is the same way you figure out your own company's ideal customer. Once you have a list of characteristics for your typical customer, you know who to look for.

> For example, if I am selling duck calls, I would most likely advertise in the magazine called Wild Fowl. Then I would see if it is possible to purchase a list of subscribers to the Wild Fowl magazine as well as a list of owners of flat bottomed boats. I'd also try to get a list of water fowl hunting licenses issued over the past year in my target area, and contact gun and rod clubs and hunting associations. With this information I would feel confident of capturing a large percentage of duck hunters. For my product, it is most likely irrelevant whether they own a house or a car, or their income or education level.

If your company services swimming pools; then, the most important information to know is if a potential customer has a pool or not. You will also want to know if they live in a house or an apartment too. A homeowner might install a pool in the future, but a non-luxury apartment dweller will rarely be your customer. Bluntly put, no pool no sale.

The bottom line: learn enough about your customer so you aren't wasting time marketing to garden nurseries if your company builds military tanks. This is important because getting a "no" time after time is frustrating and can affect your ability to enthusiastically speak with those real prospects. If you get 100 no's a day, your expectation for the next call will automatically be no. By prequalifying your contacts, you will increase your chances of getting a "maybe," which to a salesperson is an invitation to turn on the sales spigot. Maybe you can work with. No is harder.

To cut down on anemic sounding phone calls, many companies use computers for initial cold calling. When a call is connected to a person only after a customer expresses interest, it is a whole different situation for the salesperson. They have already received a "maybe" or better yet a conditional "yes" before the call is even connected. The quality of service can be better, and the order to phone call rate much higher. And, the computer could care less if a person yells or swears at it.

## Why Do Customers Buy From This Company?

There are many reasons why a customer buys from a company. Some reasons are straight forward; sometimes a customer doesn't really know why. Read more about this in Chapter 11. Below is a list of the most common motives:

## Habit

A customer buys from a company because that is what they have always done. Or, perhaps the customer was happy with the purchase of the same brand before and wants to stay with that product. At some point in time it became a habit to buy from a particular company. These are your best customers because they are not interested in comparing your price or service to others with the same intensity a new customer does. They have a certain level of trust that they will not be taken advantage of. They come in, they buy, and they get out. The transaction cost per sale is, by far, the lowest in this category. I will go into more detail about this later on.

## Location

A second reason is the physical closeness of location. For example, a lumberyard customer is a one-man-show building contractor, and the company's lumber yard is on the route from home to work. He doesn't have to make a special trip to the lumber store because it is close. He may know that another lumber yard has a reputation for being slightly cheaper than his, but it is located farther away and requires a special trip, time, and gas. The potential savings in purchasing cost are outweighed by other factors, and it's just not worth his time to make a special trip to the other place as long as this one serves him well. This is a time management issue. Material costs are usually passed on to a customer, and the contractor's time is better spent working on a job site rather than driving back and forth purchasing materials.

## Price

A third reason is price. A company offers the best price for a product. This is why some customers prefer big box stores. Big box stores are likely to carry a version of a product that fulfills the customer's requirements at that time. Because these stores are big, their purchasing power allows them to purchase their products cheaper than the smaller local store. In addition to being able to purchase items at lower cost, a company may choose to have lower profit margin, thus making the price more attractive to price conscious buyers. This strategy is sometimes used as a way to raise the utilization rate, e.g. selling with lower profit and being busier in the hopes of getting the same amount of profit dollars because of increased gross sales.

## Inventory

A fourth reason is inventory. Big box stores are usually good with price, but because they have to purchase stock for a large number of stores they can't keep all stores filled with large inventories of every product. It's common for them to have limited stock on hand. The internet is a great place to shop, but there are two limitations. One is delivery time. Sometimes a 1-2 day delivery is not fast enough. The other is that a customer can drive down to the local store and not consider their time and gas as additional cost toward their purchase, but may frown at the added shipping and packing costs for an item purchased online. If you need a large number of items, it is quite likely that you will not be able to find it all in one or even two big box stores.

> A home builder sends one of his workers to a local big box home improvement store and asks for a quantity of (500) ½"x10' metal conduit pipes. The store may carry 10-20 of them, but most likely not 500 pieces. They can special order them, but so can the builder's preferred supplier. The big box store's main customer (point 2 on this list) may not be the big construction company. Their main customer is a DIY home owner or a small contractor who does not need 500 pieces of conduit pipe at one time. They may need 10 pieces, plus a few of this item and a few of that to complete the job at hand.

This is one major reason why big box stores have not pushed local supply companies out of the market. Even if would appear so, their main customer is not exactly the same as the one for a local supply company.

## Service

The fifth reason a customer buys from a certain company is service. The customer may value the outstanding service that a company provides, has provided, or has a reputation of providing with their product. This is one area where companies are trying to separate themselves from the competition, and are using service to retain existing customers and acquire new ones. After a couple of successful sales, you may be able to turn the reason from service to habit without the customer even noticing or recognizing it.

This area is not as easy as it was a decade ago for a company to differentiate itself. In many companies, the one-time product purchase price is intentionally pushed lower than it should to acquire continuing service business. This can elevate service prices, and at some point the customer may feel, regardless of the quality of the service, that the price is simply too high.

> I know a person whose job is to call customers that have had their luxury product serviced at his employer's site. He calls a few days after the service and collects information about the customer's experience. He told me that he is increasingly hearing complaints about the price. They love the product, but feel they are taken advantage of because they are perceived as wealthy, or people who can afford the inflated price. They tell him if they had a good alternative for this work, they would go elsewhere.

## What Are the Typical Reasons Why This Company Loses Sales?

It is equally important to know and understand company weaknesses as well as strengths. Just like your company is building on its strong points, so are the competitors on theirs, and they are often using your company's weaknesses to take sales from you. You need to know how to eliminate, mitigate, or counter attack this.

One issue with gathering this data is that no one inside the company wants to talk about it because it is considered negative, or at least not a positive subject to discuss and analyze out in the open. If a company loses a sale or a customer, it is much easier to blame it on price or the individual salesperson. We were too expensive. That customer is cheap. Dave didn't have his best day. The buyer is a jerk. Sometimes that just isn't the case, and by looking deeper into the issue you may find causes that are easy and inexpensive to fix.

> Some years ago, I was buying simple steel structures for a project in the U.S. My end customer needed two identical steel stands, each about six feet tall with a base of approximately 2 feet by 3 feet. I visited a local metal fabrication shop with a set of drawings. During the meeting, I told the owner that the purpose of these structures was only to hold one 40 lb piece of equipment. The material dimensions could be relaxed and the materials themselves were pretty much free for him to choose. Furthermore, I told him it was not an urgent job; the stands were not needed for a couple of months, so he could use the job as a filler for his shop's down time. It was a perfect opportunity for him to check his back yard for scrap metal to construct these structures. He came back with a price of almost $2,000 per stand. I told him that there must be a mistake; I was

looking to pay maybe a few hundred for each stand, certainly not two thousand. The owner got roaring mad at me. I was an idiot, and why had I bothered him if I had no intention of buying? "I spent a lot of time pricing that quote." He also felt obligated to add that, "You are probably going to buy the stands from some cheap labor country like China anyway." I left his shop and I have not spoken with him since.

He may be left with the impression that it was only the price or that I was never going to buy from him anyway, but he would be wrong on both counts. It was the price to a certain extent; however, the real issue was that even though I was willing to make a joint effort to get the price lower, he never gave me an opportunity to help him. He was not interested in discussing why his price was so high, and what could be done to bring it down and still leave him profit. His obnoxious, self righteous behavior ensured that I would never try to do business with him again.

I have a feeling this same thing happens all the time. It is one of the reasons why people with good relationships do more business. If this guy was a better salesperson, he would have told me to come and take a look at his scrap yard with him to see how we could get the price lower, and engage me in coming up with a joint solution. He didn't want to do that. In his mind if I was not willing to pay the price; then, I was the jerk. That's that. I was not implying he had to fabricate the stands for free or that he couldn't make a profit. I was trying to tell him that perhaps the biggest problem we had price-wise was that the stands would be grossly overbuilt for the service they were going into. A customer doesn't want a steam shovel to make a sand castle at the beach with his two-year-old when a plastic play shovel does the job.

If you find yourself in the position where someone tells you that your product is expensive, the lead time is too long, it is too small, too big, they have seen or heard bad reviews, or whatever the reason they are giving, it should always be taken as an invitation to engage the customer in a discussion about the reasons that are holding them back from ordering. It is a perfect opportunity to ask more questions, clarify things, and try to find common ground.

- What company and product are you comparing mine to?
- What features are included, what features are not?
- Can you give me the opportunity to re-quote a comparable product?
- Are you willing to work with me on this?
- Where did you hear this?

Stressing the company's standardized mantra of service capabilities and general company features is irrelevant at this point because you are on the verge of losing the order. By talking in broad and general terms you *will* lose the sale. You need to talk in specifics and quickly find out more information. It's time to roll up your sleeves. Keep in mind that you do not have much time, or many questions to ask. If you waste your opportunity now, within a few minutes the customer will be either mentally, or both mentally and physically gone.

If you feel the sale is gone, make sure you are still polite and do not show your disappointment. The new goal is to limit damage to the current sale only. It's important to preserve the customer relationship and keep the door open for possible future business.

## Who are Your Main Competitors?

- There is no way to be successful if you do not know your competition.
- Never underestimate your competitors or their products; they are working just as hard as you. The best salespeople out there have respect for their competitors, regardless of how they may sometimes refer to them.

It is a given that your customer will compare your product to the competition. If they don't, they are the exception not the rule. When you enter into discussions with a customer, be ready to answer questions as they arise. You will not have time to look up the answers. This information must be quick and accurate. Always assume that the competitor has been educating the customer about the strong points of their product. (They might even have tried to educate them about the weaknesses of yours.) The customer will want to know if your product has the same features. If so, how do they compare? If not, why? Know your product's strong points and how they stack up against the competition. If you do not have a good rebuttal to these claims, it looks like you agree that your product is, indeed, inferior to the competition's. Or, worse yet, that you simply are not that good of a sales professional.

Other times the customer may tell you about a feature or specification of the competitor's product that they do not see in yours. It is entirely possible that it does not exist in the competitor's product either, but the customer thought it did. If you know the competitor's product, this is the perfect opportunity for you to resolve any misconceptions and make sure the customer is left with an impression that you know more, and are honest and reliable. Any salesperson that gets caught telling a fib to a customer can have a tough time winning back the customer's respect. For this reason, it is not a good idea to make up statistics and present them as facts. It is much more impressive (and long lasting) to know the facts and present them well.

You must study the competitor's product, talk to people who are using it, and try to figure out how to answer any questions when they arise. Read more about this in Chapter 4.

## Training

According to *Forbes* (August 2012), job hopping is the new normal for millennials who stay in a job for an average of a little over 2 years. I've spoken with many salespeople who expect to stay in one job for 1-3 years. This has companies reluctant to invest in exhaustive training of employees – even if data shows that it is better in the long run. Instead, they look for new hires from within the same industry: often, from a competitor. This has a real effect on training.

Normally, there are three kinds of training offered to the salesperson:

1. Highly standardized company training sessions that are carried out with groups of people.
2. Self conducted training where you find information and answers on your own.
3. Rookie salespeople are informally trained by the existing sales organization.

All three types of training have benefits and disadvantages. The most useful training will include all three.

1. Highly standardized company training is usually very good. The material is organized and presented in a coherent manner. The programs have been honed and developed into useful job related information. They are comprehensive, efficient, and time specific. Unfortunately, they often concentrate only on the technical and performance features of a product or service itself, and less on how to sell it and what obstacles you may encounter.

2. Self conducted training means learning on the job. It can be effective, but it is also expensive in the form of lost time, added frustration, and potentially lost sales and even lost customers. It takes time and requires a high level of self motivation. A newcomer may have a difficult time knowing what is right and wrong when they are acting as both student and teacher, and may not know what kind of information they will need before they find themselves in front of a customer. After 6-12 months, a salesperson might cringe at the silly

blunders they made. These mistakes could have been avoided with further training beforehand.

3. The third kind of training also happens on the job. New salespeople are taught the in's and out's of department operations by experienced salespeople. It is great for a newcomer to benefit from a veteran's experience. The downsides: information is skewed toward the opinions of the individuals providing the information and performing the training; successful people don't want to give away all their tricks; and veteran salespeople are still expected to maximize their time and make sales, and they are not necessarily benefiting from training new people.

My basic rule of thumb is to get any and all training you can. Even if it looks like you will not need the training being offered, if the company offers it and you are qualified to take it; then, take it. The more you know, the better you can do your job. Training sessions are also a great way to get to know your coworkers in a different light.

## What Kind of Support Do You Have Available to You?

Make sure you know who will be available to answer your questions and assist you when you need help. This is particularly important when you start at a new company and do not know the ropes yet. Although some companies consider the word "independent" to be synonymous with "no assistance at all," it is important that you have a network of people to rely on when you need support. The company must understand that if they do not provide help to salespeople in the trenches, they may not only lose a sale, they may also lose a customer. Most companies do realize this, and it is expected that you will seek out the advice of your manager if you need help. If you are feeling unsure of how you will be perceived, remember that the customer placing the potential order is mainly interested in the quality and timeliness of your answers, not how or where you got them. So, don't be shy using your organization.

This raises another important question regarding support. Is sales an individual or team sport? How much should you help your sales colleagues, or them you, when sales is, even if no one says it aloud, a competition? Almost every salesperson wants to shine as the best in the office. The corner office, the title of sales director or VP of sales, more money, and respect are the prize. How will helping you, the rival salesperson who also wants the big office, benefit them? There's an inherent problem when everyone is racing for the same personal goal. There is no easy solution; however, you better keep in mind that no one is going to put all their marbles out for you no matter how nice they are because knowledge is power.

**Other Questions to Ask**

At some point you will find yourself in front of a customer, and they will ask you questions related to your company. In addition to product information, you will need to know the answers. Remember, part of your job is to make certain that the customer has no doubt about your company and believes in the capability of your company to execute potential orders. Most of this information is exchanged informally while chit-chatting with the customer.

- When was the company founded?
- Who owns the company? Is it privately or publicly held?
- Who are the company's largest customers?
- What is the company's personnel turnover rate?
- Is the company growing, shrinking, or staying the same?
- What is your policy regarding …

Compare the company's last three years of financial reports. The *Wall Street Journal* (June 2015) reported that the average 10K filing contains more words than some famous literary works, so there is a lot of information available if you take the time to look. If these are not readily available, ask your manager where you can find this information. Keep in mind that if you work for a smaller company and your manager is the owner, they may not be willing to share this information.

There are other questions you should ask as well that require a high level of discretion. Learn this information quickly, quietly, and tactfully and use it with caution.

## What Is the Company's Unwritten Performance?

When you join a new company as their sales representative, you get handed a list of 300 active customers as well as another list of 500 dormant or one time customers in your territory. You are excited and call one of your biggest potential customers (A common mistake for new hires – you should practice with ones where you have nothing to lose) and it goes something like this:

> You introduce yourself as the new guy handling their business. You are polite and helpful, and tell the customer how you will take good care of them. The customer, on the other hand, tells you that you are the fourth guy from your company presenting themselves as "his contact" in the last six months. He continues, "Your company never responds in a timely fashion, and deliveries are always late." He ends with, "Why should you be any different? It's your company that's the problem." Furthermore, while your predecessors were not servicing this customer's needs they found another company they like, and are not looking to change vendors. Your existing account list just shrunk by one, and you had nothing to do with it.

This doesn't mean that you can't reestablish a relationship with this customer. What it does mean is that it will take a lot more effort and time. You will have to work, work, work, and one day an opportunity will open and that will be your chance.

You need to know what you are dealing with, and your manager will not voluntarily give up the unpleasant factual information about your position. His goal is to keep you motivated, and part of this is not telling you that the three guys before you quit or were transferred to other positions within a ten month period. Again, I stress proceed with caution. Do not make this a point of contention in your job, but do quickly, quietly, and tactfully take note of the historical information that impacts your sales relationships.

In the case above, you would most likely do what everyone else does. You would throw your predecessor under the bus and assure this customer that you will be different from the others. "Just give me a chance to show it!" The big issue at hand, though, is if the guys before you ruined all the potential customer relationships within your assigned territory or just that one?

Here are additional questions for you to ponder:

- What are the other unwritten rules?
- Who makes the decisions?
- What is the decision making criteria?
- How much latitude do you have with pricing?
- Delivery?
- What else should I be asking?

## Your Product

If you have a product to sell, it is obvious that you should know that product inside out. This is an area where standardized company training programs do a good job. Companies performing standardized training have identified the importance of their salespeople knowing their product. If you work for one of these companies, congratulations, you have a jumpstart on the questions below. If your company does not offer standardized training though, it is still imperative to your future that you educate yourself. Be prepared to spend quite a bit of your own time learning this stuff. You can't look at it as wasted time. It's an investment in faster results.

If your company has hundreds or even thousands of products, by no means are you expected to know everything about each and every one. At least from the company's point of view. However, when you flip the view, a customer may not expect you to know absolutely everything, but they will expect you to know at least something about all your company products. They will assume that you have been trained. That's just the way it is. If you are in a position where you only have a limited amount of products to learn, learn them really well. Quite frankly, it does not always take much knowledge to be a salesperson. Sometimes just knowing a bit more than the customer, or being able to read the info sheet is enough.

Here are some of the product related questions you should answer:

## What Is the Product Development History of This Product?

You may wonder why this is useful. Over the years, I have used this information more times than I can count; mainly for rebutting misinformation planted with the customer by a competitor. Often times a competitor will have old information about your product. They either didn't update their data or the old data is more suitable to their needs: winning an order for the same sale you are bidding. Remember, as mentioned before, your competitor is working as hard as you are for an order, and not everyone will play nice. Some salespeople will use any tool at their disposal, such as identifying the perceived weakness in your product while playing up the good points of their own. This is the reality of sales.

Company E makes cell phones. Model 4 of the phone had some bugs well known amongst the customer base. For the sake of our example, let's say the camera didn't work like it should. A new model came out a year ago, Model 5, where most of the issues were fixed. It would not be uncommon if Company E's competitors mentioned to potential customers that *Company E has had a big problem with the cameras in their phones*, and they do not know if it has been fixed yet or not. Here's the kicker: they know. They know very well, but they are planting a seed of doubt in the mind of a potential customer. They might even go so far as to tell the customer that if that problem exists and Company E hasn't done anything about it, they wonder what other problems there are with that phone. If you are selling phones for Company E, you need to have enough knowledge about the product to tell the customer that *yes, there was a slight wrinkle with the Model 4 phone, but those issues were fixed with the Model 5 phone that came out last year.*

## What Is an Ideal Customer or Application for This Product?

Most products have that one application or use where they simply are at their best. Those are the sales cases you should never lose. However, it is tough if you do not know what that perfect fit is. Your manager should be able to teach you how to identify their ideal customer, and this information should be easy to get from other salespeople in the company.

## What Are the Main Competitor's Products That Compete With This Product?

Know your competition for each and every product. It may not always be the same company, so it should be evaluated on a case by case basis.

What is the customer looking for?

> A car is a product, but all cars are not the same. Furthermore, not all cars offered within the same company fill the same need. If I ask what car is a competitor for BMW, I bet many people would say Audi or Mercedes. If I ask what is a competitor for the Dodge Viper, they might answer Chevy Corvette. Not all Chevy's are competitors for all Dodges, only certain products. A customer looking at a Viper or Corvette may not be looking for a pickup or four door sedan. Their *need* is different.

Collect this data and make a list. Update it as you receive information, so that it stays current.

## What Are the Top Competing Products for This Product?

As said earlier, there is an overproduction of just about any product in the market. This is why I would almost guarantee that whatever your product is, there are competing products. You need to know what those products are because they are the ones that can take away your sales. Study their features well, and try to find out how the competition is selling their products.

## When an Order or Sale for This Product Is Lost or Won, What Are the 5 Main Reasons That Customers Give?

You and your company have figured this one out. It is available information. From now on, you need to be prepared to predict these items before you lose the order. Always know how to answer those "sale killing" questions.

Most companies have comparison sheets to compare different products for their sales use. If your company does not have one; then, create a list of your own. These are useful when talking to a customer on the phone or in person. Just about any time you can pull out the list and start explaining where and why your product is superior when compared to the competition.

## How is Our Pricing Compared With the Competitions? Do We Offer Discounts? Who Determines the Price Level?

Many of today's customers are price sensitive, so you need to know the competitions' prices. Don't know? Ask the customer what your competitor quoted. They will usually tell you. The answer might be, "Your price is 20% more than Competitor X." If you feel uncomfortable about asking, think of the following situation:

> You walk into one of the two major pet stores to find a flea collar for your dog. A salesperson tells you about the benefits of the collar and asks if you want one. Having visited the other major pet store the day before, you tell the sales person that their flea collar is $10 more than the other store.

See, it's almost instinctual to answer. The customer wants to tell you because they see it as an opportunity for you to match the price, beat the price, or say there is nothing to be done. One just has to be able to ask the right questions.

Unless you own the business, there may not be much that you can do about setting the price. But, if you know the market pricing of your product and a customer tells you that, "DDD brand is one-half the price of yours," and you know that it is not, you will be able to clarify if the competitor is offering an equivalent product and restate that you are offering a good price for your product.

The salesperson in the flea collar example above can thank the customer for pointing out the price discrepancy between competitive products and their own ("I'm glad you brought it up ... "); then, explain how that particular collar lasts 12 months versus the competitor's product that lasts only eight months.

Always keep in mind that when the customer is in front of you and is talking to you, it is your "face time." Use it to your advantage.

A small discount is often a good way to develop a new customer.

> I recently visited a major American motorcycle showroom to buy some parts. I could not help but admire how the salesperson handled my purchase. When I walked to the parts counter with my list, the very first thing he asked was if I was in the computer system. It wasn't asked for the ease of transaction; it was a way for him to find out quickly whether I was a repeat customer, infrequent customer, or a new customer with the potential of becoming a regular customer. He rang me up; then, offered a small discount. Why? He wanted me to leave with a good feeling, which he achieved. If I ever need more parts, they hope I will think of them first, which they also achieved. This was a perfect sales transaction.

Other questions to ask:

- What are the upper and lower limitations of this product? (capacity, temperature, dimensions, motor size, resolution, speed, output, etc.)
- Are our competitors' products in any way better than ours? (price, delivery time, physical size, color selection, higher temperature, more seating capacity, etc.)
- Who are our best or biggest references for this product, and can we use their names?

Think of any other questions that will help you know the product you are selling. Write down some of the more common questions from customers and use time during your quieter days to find the perfect answers.

## Know Your Product Applications

You have to know how your product is used, and you have to learn it quickly. This includes the special terminology used in the industry. Keep in mind that the terminology, even in the same language, varies from one region or country to another.

Knowing your product's applications directly helps you with sales; obviously. It also helps you with one of the most important skills you will need in your sales career: time management. You should be spending the majority of your time on projects that are most likely to turn into an order. If you know the best applications for your product and how it has been applied to solve customer needs and problems in the past, you can use this to your advantage.

Customers in the same industry typically have similar problems. Problems bother customers and cost them money. If you know your product performs well in the bottling end of a soda pop factory, you know it will also work well for other companies that bottle similar products. It is worth your time and effort to start targeting those potential customers. On the flip side, if a customer contacts you wanting a product that helps them bottle propane, you will know it may not be worth your time to pursue that quotation because it clearly falls outside the parameters of your product. No doubt if one spends enough time learning how propane is bottled, it could turn into a sale. Again, the big question is if it is worth the time invested. Especially when there are companies out there who have an out-of-the-box product that can do the job.

## Expanding Your Customer Base Within the Same Company

If you sell a product or service to a customer with multiple locations within the same territory, it is the perfect opportunity to expand your relationship with that company. Other locations may be experiencing the same problems, but have not solved them. You should be working to roll your product into those sites, as well. If your product resolved the problem and is saving the customer money, they will appreciate it. They will appreciate it with more than just that one order's worth as long as your product keeps performing well.

The bigger the problem and the bigger the savings, the more likely they are to share the information between plants or locations. However, never take for granted this is happening. You have to be proactive in presenting your solution to the customer's other plants or locations; you can never rely only on internal word of mouth. You would assume that if a customer has multiple plants that they are talking amongst each other. Most of the time this is true, but sometimes they are not. It depends how big of an issue the problem was perceived for the customer. Over the years, I have also met customers where different sites are competing so fiercely with each other to stay in existence that they sometimes don't share advances within their own company. I'm not saying they purposely do it; sometimes information just doesn't seem to flow, and you have to make sure it does.

# 2.

# SALES PROCESS: THE LADDER APPROACH

If you ask me which chapter you should read twice, this is it. Over the years, I have discovered a sales process I refer to as *The Ladder Approach*. There are 12 distinct steps, or rungs, every sales cycle follows. The rungs of the ladder create a logical progression of tasks; basically, a step by step checklist of questions and related work that need to be answered.

All sales begin with a customer with a need. Can your product or service satisfy that need?

1. **Do you have a suitable product to fulfill a need that the customer has?** *[handwritten: Tinnitus product]*

    Can your product solve the customer's problem? If not, your chances for success with this particular sale are low. Remember that a need can also be a perceived one, and not immediately apparent to you.

2. **Are you able to identify what exactly the customer needs?**

    If you are selling windows and the customer is looking for windows, it appears that Rung 1 has been satisfied. Now, do you know if the customer wants aluminum, vinyl, wood, metal, or some other material frames for their windows? How many panes, what sizes, colors, etc.? Does your product actually meet the need, or are you trying to convince the customer that his needs should be slightly modified to fit your product instead of your product fitting his need?

3. **Can you demonstrate your capability to fulfill the potential order?**

   Have you done this before? Do you have similar references that you can show the customer? If the customer wants a roof replaced, chances are they will want to know that you have done roofing before. If you are a language teacher who has never roofed, the probability of getting the order are low.

4. **Does the customer seem like they have a positive or at least a neutral opinion of your company?**

   Has your company had any dealings with the customer before? Have they been either positive or at least neutral? If you have done business with this customer in the past and your performance was not up to par, or in some other way left a bad impression with the customer, this order may not come your way.

   Salespeople don't always consider the impact that personnel movement within an industry has on their job. New people bring their established opinions with them into a customer organization, and that opinion can be transferred to others within the company. As a consequence, people you have never met may have a strong opinion about you or your product long before you meet.

5. **Can you produce a bid on time?**

   Customers should ask for a quotation in writing. There are cases where a verbal quote and commitment from the customer are enough, but unless this is an OTC (over the counter) deal I would recommend that you do not do verbal deals and make sure everything is in writing. Otherwise, there are too many things that can go wrong. The customer and you may remember differently what was agreed upon, and it will cause problems later. Make sure everything about the deal is clear to both parties in advance. This way, there is a much better chance of developing a good and lasting customer.

6. **Can you meet the customer's price?**

If the customer has indicated a price level, can you meet it or convince them to increase (or lower!) their budget? If you can't meet these requirements, this order may go to someone else.

Why convince a customer to lower their budget? If you truly are the cheapest gig in town, you may want to create a lower price expectation to weed out some competitors by setting the price expectation to suit you.

7. **Can you answer the customer's questions in a timely manner?**

One thing that really upsets a customer that is ready to order is not getting or getting poor answers from a seller. It is a common reason why at the last minute (or so it seems to the oblivious seller) the customer changes his mind about a vendor and orders from someone else. The seller, who thought they were in the driver's seat, is completely floored when it happens.

Answering customer questions quickly and accurately can easily be turned into a competitive edge during the sales cycle that is well worth your time and effort.

8. **Can you find out and eliminate the customer's obstacles for ordering?**

The customer needs the product or service they are trying to buy. However, there can be obstacles that prevent them from ordering all together, or ones that are in the way of them just ordering from you. These obstacles can include anything from your contact not having the authority to make a final decision to buy, to not having a clear understanding of what it is that they want. Maybe they want a product, but can't really afford it, or their priorities have changed. Yesterday the customer was shopping for a television, and today the washing machine broke. Now, the TV purchase is put on hold because the TV funds have to be used on a washing machine. The store or supplier may stay the same or change. Oftentimes a customer does not tell the seller what the obstacles are. Sometimes they hint at it, especially if you ask.

For example, you are negotiating a house painting contract with a customer.

"You have the price. You've talked with some of our customers and know we can do a good job for you," you say. "Can you tell me what is preventing you from signing the house painting contract right now?" The customer may haltingly tell you that she and her husband have a difference of opinion about the color. You could continue, "Is that it? If we can solve that right now, do we have a deal?" You now know exactly how to proceed with the sale – maybe you get some boards and paint both colors on them and lead the discussions. Unless you mess it up, you should know that this is your deal.

### 9. Can you negotiate and execute a contract?

There should always be a contract. The base for the contract will be your written quotation. People enter verbal contracts all the time, and have problems all the time, as well. Even for simple, straightforward (or so you think) items, type up a simple contract of what was discussed verbally, and include the key points such as price and delivery.

I was travelling during a particularly stormy winter. My wife contacted a local contractor we knew for snow plowing services while I was gone. The contractor called and offered a good price, and they made a verbal agreement over the phone. The contractor told her if she paid cash every time he came, so he didn't have to bother with billing, he would charge $60 per storm. During my trip there were four storms. After the last storm, my wife went to pay like she had for the previous three. When she offered the money, the contractor refused and said, "Don't pay me yet; I haven't decided how much I'm going to charge you." After a couple of days, he contacted my wife and told her he wanted an additional $200. Since then, we heard that the contractor was being sued and had financial problems. Perhaps he thought he could squeeze and additional $200 from us, or perhaps he just did not remember what was agreed.

My point here is that at the time of a verbal agreement, conditions are one way. But, they can change – sometimes very quickly. When faced with serious problems, people's behavior can change dramatically. This is why there should always be a written contract in place. Issues like this are much more common than you think. An email stating the main points of an agreement will go a long way.

## 10. Can you get internal support for your bid within the customer's organization?

Many salespeople like to stick only to their contacts at the customer, but the fact is if you want to make a sale, you need to make sure that more than one person is your supporter. Keep in mind that a buying decision can be made by more than one person as a team effort. Your job is to convince as many members of this team as you can that your product or service is superior.

It doesn't just happen in large companies. If a couple is shopping for a new car, it's quite common for the rookie salesperson to concentrate only on the husband even if the new car is for the wife, and she holds the ultimate decision making power. I've learned that no matter what I am selling, if there is more than one person buying, I make the effort to get them all on board. If you don't get them all on your side, pay attention to who is for you and who is against you.

## 11. Can you close the sale?

There are four kinds of buyers.

a) The buyer who has already decided what they will buy and where they will buy it. This group is relatively easy to deal with; all you have to do is not to screw up and you have the sale.

b) Buyers that are torn between two or three equally good alternatives. The customer is willing and ready, but they need a slight push to go with your offering. The key here is that they have already prequalified your product as one of the alternatives. Good sales closers are at their best in front of this group.

c) Buyers who are strongly leaning toward another product, but are still somewhat intrigued by your offering. Here a good closer may be able to change the almost inevitable, but the percentage for success is low.

d) Buyers who have already decided to buy from someone else. This is the same group as *a* above, but with this group the decision is against your product or service. A good closer will quickly determine this situation is a low chance one, and move his main efforts on to the next customer. But, he will also do this graciously, and leave the customer with a good impression.

## 12. Can you deliver as promised?

Delivery is not always considered a part of the sales cycle, but in my opinion this completes the sales cycle. It is important that things go well, so that you can potentially sell to this person or company again or use them as a reference.

This is basic knowledge that many salespeople are unable to dissect. Often they go through these steps without really thinking. It is good practice to analyze your prospective sales cases, and make sure you have not missed any of these steps. A good sales professional understands the process, and identifies where in the process a quotation is at any given time.

Keep in mind that every process needs a process owner. If you are not the owner of that process, it will be someone else. It can be your customer, or worse yet, your competitor.

# THE SALES PROCESS FROM A CUSTOMER POINT OF VIEW

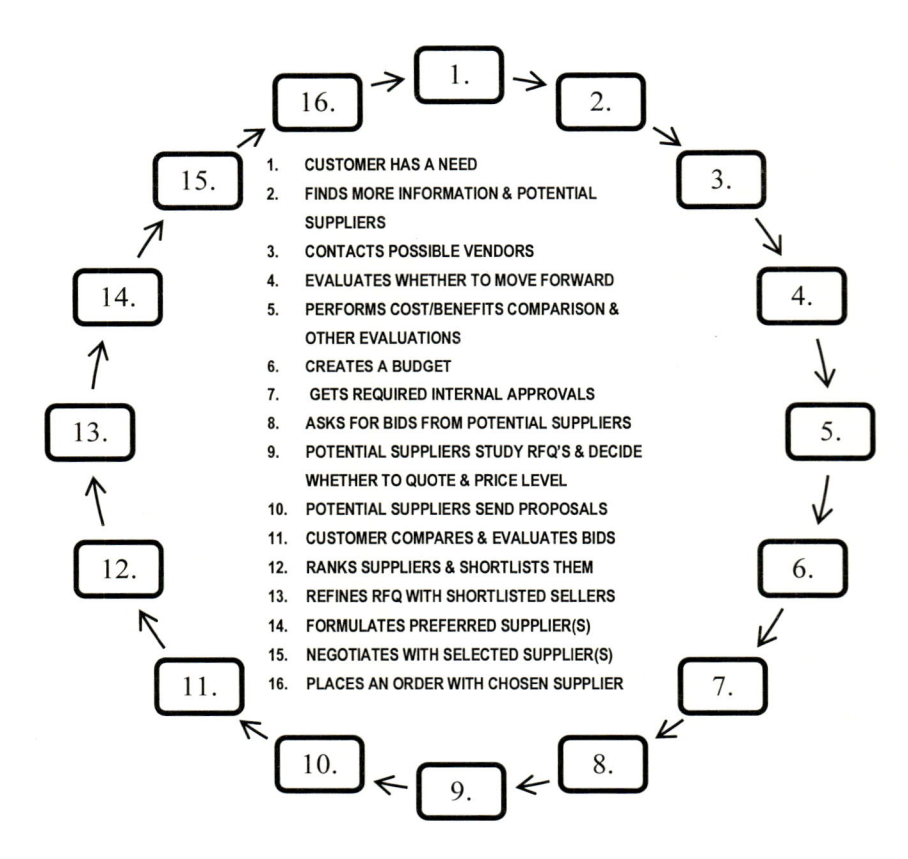

1. CUSTOMER HAS A NEED
2. FINDS MORE INFORMATION & POTENTIAL SUPPLIERS
3. CONTACTS POSSIBLE VENDORS
4. EVALUATES WHETHER TO MOVE FORWARD
5. PERFORMS COST/BENEFITS COMPARISON & OTHER EVALUATIONS
6. CREATES A BUDGET
7. GETS REQUIRED INTERNAL APPROVALS
8. ASKS FOR BIDS FROM POTENTIAL SUPPLIERS
9. POTENTIAL SUPPLIERS STUDY RFQ'S & DECIDE WHETHER TO QUOTE & PRICE LEVEL
10. POTENTIAL SUPPLIERS SEND PROPOSALS
11. CUSTOMER COMPARES & EVALUATES BIDS
12. RANKS SUPPLIERS & SHORTLISTS THEM
13. REFINES RFQ WITH SHORTLISTED SELLERS
14. FORMULATES PREFERRED SUPPLIER(S)
15. NEGOTIATES WITH SELECTED SUPPLIER(S)
16. PLACES AN ORDER WITH CHOSEN SUPPLIER

This is the sales process from the customer's point of view. As you can see, the salesperson is not involved in many of the process steps. That is why it is so important that the seller gathers as much information as possible.

# 3.

# THE SALES PERSONALITY

It is important to know *what* you are selling. It is equally important to know *how* you are selling. In the *Harvard Business Review*, Steve W. Martin reports "The Seven Personality Traits of Top Salespeople" (June 27, 2011). Martin interviewed thousands of top performing salespeople and administered personality tests to 1,000 of them to create a list of common personality traits found in the participants. These qualities emerged as significant indicators:

1. Modesty
2. Conscientiousness
3. Achievement orientation
4. Curiosity
5. Lack of gregariousness
6. Lack of discouragement
7. Lack of self consciousness.

Mr. Martin's study confirms what I have seen in the field. What I really like is that this study backs my claim that a good salesperson is not the guy who walks into the room with a dozen jokes, tries to be best buddies with everyone, or is plain old pushy: the guy who always says yes or won't take no for an answer.

I've always believed that you make your own luck by working hard. Luck follows hard work. Although someone can possess some of these inherent traits, there are no natural born salespeople. Every salesperson has to develop their knowledge and talent to do well in this job.

There are billions of people on this earth. In your sales career you will come across people who like you and people who you like. Those meetings and interactions will be nice and easy. However, no matter how hard you try, you will also come across people who are completely turned off by you. They just do not like dealing with you. Quite often you will not know why. Perhaps it is the way you comb your hair, the words you use to speak, the clothes you wear, maybe you remind them of someone they don't like, or who knows what else? They just don't like you, and you will have to learn to tolerate it. Some customers will forgive your personal flaws (their opinion, not mine) and deal with you anyway. Others will not. When these situations arise, you must remain positive, calm, and not let your frustration take over. Always keep in mind that you are the salesperson and they are the customer, and they have the liberty to choose any salesperson they wish.

I have met plenty of people who did not seem to like me. No matter how many times this happens it does not get easier. Most likely because it is my persona that they don't like. Still, I have always thought that the earlier I know this, the better. I can then evaluate whether it is worth investing a lot of time in that particular quote. On the other hand, I have met plenty of people who I seem to click with right away. Working with them is fun and easy, and many of those quotations somehow end up with an order.

Knowing this will happen to you at some point, you should understand that your goal is not to make everyone like you; your goal is to do your job to the best of your ability and earn the customer's trust that your opinion is honest and valuable. This will be your best strategy to overcome situations like this. Let's take another look at Martin's personality traits and interpret them within real life selling experience.

1. <u>Modesty</u>. You are not the only piece in the sales puzzle. Pushing your own agenda for ego's sake and excluding the other players in the game is a good way to distance possible decision makers in the

customer's organization and in your own. This is especially true for the salesperson who just will not take no for an answer. Stretching the patience of a busy customer that has made a clear decision quickly turns obnoxious, and the issue becomes not only losing an order, but losing a customer altogether.

> I was traveling in the midwest with one of my salespeople. He was truly a student of the don't-take-no-for-an-answer sales philosophy. He was rushing to get to his bank before it closed at 5:00pm, knowing there was no way we could make it before 5:30pm. He called the branch manager and requested them to stay open one hour later, so he could come in and complete his transaction. They said no.
>
> * * *
>
> Some years ago, I had a young sales colleague concentrating on a certain business area. He received almost no orders, but it was never his fault. He kept pointing out flaws in everyone else, but himself. He was convinced he could sell ice in the South Pole; his skills were so marvelous. The only problem, in his view, was that all the customers were stupid and just did not understand.

Based on what I have seen over the years, the more noise a salesperson makes about themselves, the more excuses they tend to have for their lackluster performance. These people are never the highest performers.

2. <u>Conscientiousness</u>. Be thorough and accurate in your work. Be dependable and accountable. Follow through on promises, and take responsibility for getting a sale.

   The people belonging to this category are "all-in" in their sales career. They do not look at the clock or the calendar. They want to win, and they are willing to work for it. This is where clashes begin. Unfortunately, no great success comes without sacrifice, and it is often hobbies, friends, and family who end up giving. This is sometimes misunderstood as aligning priorities, which it is not. Because this personality is "all in," they are afraid that missing one email or phone call may cause them to lose a sale. And, it may very well be the case. I have often wondered if it would be possible to team up two of these folks who could learn to completely trust each other, so they could actually enjoy some time off every now and then.

3. <u>Achievement Orientation</u>. Keep your eye on the prize: winning the sale. Analyze what you need to do and who you have to convince to get this sale. Make a To Do list and keep on top of it. If you are a person who knows at any time where you are with your budget as well as where all your coworkers are in comparison to you, you are one of these people.

4. <u>Curiosity</u>. Actively ask questions and listen to your customer. Be interested in finding out what they want, why they want it, and respond to that need. Don't be so caught up in your own presentation and what you want to say that you don't hear. People in this category are never too proud to admit they do not know something. Once they learn it, they know it. More about this in Chapter 11.

5. <u>Lack of Gregariousness</u>. There is a pervasive opinion that to be successful, a sales person has to be the most outgoing and social person in the room. This is not true. Your best customers are not looking for someone to entertain them. They are looking for an expert they trust to help them solve a problem. Their jobs may depend on it. The salesperson that can command respect and convince the customer that their advice is sound will be more successful at making sales than the one who walks in with the best wit and humor. Think hard about this. If you are the customer and

your boss will be scrutinizing how your purchasing decision affects productivity and profits, who would you rather buy from?

> My (Finnish) manager and I were on our way to a first meeting at a company (a metal fabricating company) in New York State. The first thing out of my manager's mouth before even introducing himself, "Where's the toilet?" he asked. The customer pointed and my manager took a couple of steps toward the door, turned, and felt compelled to explain why he needed to go. "For the past fifteen minutes I've been telling Timo to pull over anywhere so I can piss, but he wouldn't." He was always trying to be funny. This is certainly a way to leave a lasting impression on a company, but I wouldn't recommend it.

6. <u>Lack of Discouragement</u>. Don't be discouraged when you lose an order. Regardless of how good a salesperson you are, you will not win them all. Every time you find yourself in front of the customer, it's an opportunity to get to know the people within that organization. You have learned something about the competitor: their sales style and product offering. Next time, you will know that much more about what you are up against. It's a good time to define a strategy. How will you attack this situation if it happens again?

> I had a seasoned salesperson working for me. He had a quality I always admired. When he lost an order, he would mourn the loss for one cup of coffee's worth. While drinking his coffee, he would think about the important events of the quote and decide what had happened. When the cup was empty, it was time to move on to the next quote. If you can train yourself to do this, you will be successful.

7. <u>Lack of Self Consciousness</u>. Become confident in your presentation skills. Some people are naturally comfortable speaking in front of crowds or groups of people while others' hearts palpitate at the thought. This is such an important part of selling that if you are one of the latter folks, you need to find a way to get over it. Sometimes when you are forced to do it anyway it helps, but there are people who will never get over their fear. If you are one of those people, you will have to think hard about how you will proceed. Maybe your career will be in telephone sales, or other positions where you do not have to speak in front of people. Just make sure you give it your all before you give up.

> My wife used to be terrified of speaking up in meetings or, heaven forbid, standing in front of an audience. When we moved overseas, she was offered a position as a corporate trainer. The job entailed speaking in front of groups of mid managers and sessions with executives. It was a frightening proposition. She still accepted the offer because she decided that having to perform the same task three to five times per day five days a week would desensitize her to the fear. The first meetings weren't the easiest or smoothest, but day by day she improved and is no longer paralyzed by her fear and is at ease in front of people.

We all make mistakes. An important skill is to either recover from a mistake or forget it and move on. If you made a small mistake in your product presentation, do not dwell on it. If you move on with this customer, you can make a correction later. If you dwell on it, you can lose your composure and mess up the entire presentation.

# 4.

# A CLOSER LOOK AT COMPETITOR INFORMATION

## Who or What Are You Competing Against?

Do you know who you are competing against? You may ask, "If I don't get the sale, what difference does it make to me who gets it?" It does matter. This entire subject is a cornerstone in any sales career, and it should be learned as early as possible.

You need to know your competition. Competition can mean different things in different situations. Competition can be an individual sales manager, a company, a product or service, and sometimes it can be a completely different solution to a customer's problem. You need to listen to your customers and ask the right questions to find out their preferences, so you can change your offering and strategy accordingly. At all times make sure you are competitive against the front runner.

Traditionally, competition is used to mean other companies, products, or services out in the market place that all could, at least to some extent, fulfill the customer's need at that time. The key point is "at least to some extent are equivalent." We all know that the products being compared are not always equal at all, and it is your job to educate the customer about the benefits of your product or service over other ones.

Below is an example of competition in the form of a completely different solution to a customer's problem:

You are a contractor, and a customer tells you that they have decided to build a new house. They tell you that they are talking with two other contractors, as well. They want you to quote a complete package, including land and building the new house on it. They may not specifically tell you that they have alternative avenues, but you should be objective and consider each of the alternatives yourself. Realistically, the customer has at least two other options. One is to build an addition to their existing home if they have one. The second one is to purchase a new or almost new house already on the market. Both of these options are detrimental to your cause if you are only offering a new house on a piece of land. Start the qualification process and probe these alternatives, and the customer's reactions to them. You do not want to spend a lot of time looking for a piece of land and making proposals only to be told later on that, "Sorry, we found a nice house in an established neighborhood we liked, and decided to buy it on the spot."

Think like the customer and expand your idea of the term "competitor." Search for alternative ways you would look to satisfy your need if you were in the customer's situation; then, plan how you will handle each situation.

## Analyzing the Competition

When you are competing with products or services that can also be provided by other companies, you are in classic competition mode. Not all the products need to be exactly the same, but they fill the same need.

You must answer to the competition's strongest points and, quite frankly, use their weakest points to your advantage.

# A CLOSER LOOK AT COMPETITOR INFORMATION

Let's say that I am in the dumpster rental business and I have 100 buckets. I have a lot of smaller competitors, each with 10-15 buckets. I can almost guarantee that I will always be able to deliver a bucket. This is clearly my strong point, and my entire marketing campaign revolves around bucket availability. My competition, on the other hand, is almost guaranteed to run out of buckets at one time or another during a busy season. They may be able to negotiate and juggle schedules to a certain extent to keep a customer happy, but they can't do it all the time. If a new customer calls and asks for a bucket because their usual supplier is out, guess what my pitch is?

The competition's strong point, though, may just be those negotiating and juggling skills because they always seem able to pull a rabbit out of their hat at the last minute. My weakness may be my inability to pick up or deliver buckets at the *exact time* the customer wants because I have to plan my driving routes to cover the numerous buckets that are spread over several towns.

Make a table to analyze your competitors. Include capacity, skills, performance, resources, delivery time, price, and any other important variables. This table is your sales compass. It will show you what you need to concentrate on when competing with company A or company B on the same bid.

Keeping this table nearby will remind you how to sharpen the arguments for your product. A table like this is also useful when you are talking on the phone.

## Competitor Sales Styles

Just like individuals, companies tend to develop sales styles of their own too. This probably happens in an organization because decisions are made by the same people who dole out the same or similar advice to their salespeople. Company sales styles can be subtle and rely on the individual salesperson's technique, or the style can be structured and leave little room for individual approaches. Some companies consider their style part of their brand.

Figuring out how the competition sells can take years. Experienced salespeople may feel proprietary over this hard earned information when it comes to sharing with new hires. In the sales professional's mind, rights to this information equals better than average performance, which leads to job security and possible job promotions. Sharing needs to benefit everyone.

One way to implement information-sharing is through a 10-15 minute competitor review during monthly sales meetings. Every month, the person responsible for keeping up and collecting this information can make a short presentation of the latest findings about competitors or the latest information on all competitors in general. The same person can make the presentation from month-to-month, or the responsibility can travel from one salesperson to another. Sometimes people are more open to sharing information when they are recognized as the originator. If your sales department doesn't do this, maybe you can do something similar with a coworker over lunch or after work. You may find that you both know something that you can share, and after lunch you both are better positioned to get those sales.

I have come across at least six major sales styles over the years:

1. The low cost supplier that makes price reductions, one after another, causing other suppliers to be dropped from the race just like that.

# A CLOSER LOOK AT COMPETITOR INFORMATION 51

They do not seem to have a floor in their pricing. This supplier might get information about other bidder's prices through their contacts at the company, or it is just their sales style.

2. The supplier that presents a thick specification detailing the scope of their offer and may allude to the fact that this and that are included in the price, but after purchasing the customer finds out the hard way that all items were not included. The supplier refers to the contract signed by the customer stating that all their obligations have, indeed, been met.

3. An entire sales style built on badmouthing competitors and talking so much negative trash about them that the customer actually starts avoiding those companies in case some of it is true. Unfortunately, if people hear trash-talking enough, they will start doubting the party being talked against. Look at political campaigns. Negativity *does* work in today's society; hopefully, not tomorrow's.

4. Reference based sales where the supplier points out one great reference after another, and in this way attempts to convince the customer that they are the most experienced supplier in this field. They like to point out to a customer that, "There may be less pricey companies out there, but they definitely aren't as good as we are."

5. More or less, a copy-cat company rides the coattails of the perceived market leader by creating an impression that the quality of their product is the same as the leading company's product. We have the same … as … we buy the same components as … we use the same subcontractors as …

6. Companies that seem to work tirelessly toward quoting the customer's exact specifications. These are often large corporations where individual power is limited, and they know how to perform

risk analysis on each quotation. They typically play it safe and are often criticized for being expensive.

# PART II:
# THE SALES CALL

# 5.

# THE PRODUCTIVE SALES CALL OR MEETING

This chapter goes over the preparation and execution of a successful sales call or meeting. It concentrates on efficient use of time and getting maximum results by utilizing good planning.

It is important to set realistic goals for a call or meeting. Remember, it is very rare that you call someone and they tell you during the first call, "Sure, I'll buy one!" It is more likely you will make dozens of calls and hit one *maybe* every now and then. Out of those many maybe's you are able to get a few orders. In part, this is a game of statistics. The more calls you make, the more maybe's you should get. The more maybe's, the more sales.

If you plan your sales calls and meetings like you plan other important events, you are more likely to achieve good results. Preparation is important. The more you do it, the more natural it will become. It's still important to analyze your performance periodically, so you are constantly improving.

When Boston Sales Challenge conducts a company-specific training session on sales there is a minimum of two to three days of preparation, sometimes four to five, for a two day seminar.

## Preparing for the Call or Meeting

Just like any other task or job, you need to make sure you are well prepared before your sales call or meeting. Every call and every meeting is an opportunity to set the groundwork or build upon an existing relationship for a sale. Make sure you do not miss out on any one of them.

There are three high level outcomes for a meeting or call:

1. The outcome is positive
2. The outcome is indifferent. It was not positive, but neither was it negative
3. The outcome is negative

You could fall into category (3) if you are not well prepared for a call or meeting. Why? You didn't engage the customer because you were so busy talking you didn't take time to listen. Perhaps your lack of knowledge didn't convince the customer to buy from you, and also convinced them that they don't need what you are offering. Maybe they don't, or maybe you did a poor job of explaining what it is you are offering. I cannot tell you how often I get a phone call where I must ask the caller, "Can you tell me in plain English what exactly are you are trying to sell me?" You have to avoid this outcome any way you can.

> Note:
>
> Your goals will determine how you prepare for your call.

Before calling a customer, have a clear objective for the call. Think this out in advance. What are you hoping to achieve? Possible objectives can be staying in touch with the customer, or trying to set up an appointment for a visit to make a product presentation. Perhaps your goal is for them to visit your website for more information. Whatever the objective, it is what should guide the preparation. If you don't prepare and you just fly by the seat of your pants with no direction, you can end up with no results, or worse, with negative results.

Objectives for a successful sales call:

- Keep in touch: say hello, we have not spoken in a long time, I am still here if you need me
- Find out what is happening with the customer; set up a meeting for a product demonstration
- Make contacts, find out who handles your product at purchasing
- Give the customer a brief description of your product and a website address where they can find more information
- Find out where the company is currently buying their product and why
- Introduce yourself as their contact person for this type of product at your company
- What is the process for scheduling a product presentation to a group of people (like the purchasing team)
- Find out more about a project, referring to an email your company or you received asking for a proposal
- Respond to a voice mail

Just like the rest of the sales process, you must take an analytical approach. You need to describe why you are contacting the customer. Be careful not to call just for the sake of calling when you don't have anything else to do because these calls can be a nuisance and interpreted as bothering people.

Next, you have to set a goal for the call. Once you reach your goal there is no need to continue the call, unless the customer keeps up the conversation of course. Once the goal is reached, end the phone call or meeting. It is very easy to close the conversation by saying something like, "Ok, I'll see you on Thursday the 9$^{th}$ at 2:00 pm in your office. Now I will let you get back to work, thanks for your time."

Resist the urge to keep talking just because you have the customer's ear. Overstaying your welcome can leave a bad impression for wasting time.

It is not a good thing to get a reputation for being the salesperson no one can politely get rid of on the phone. You've had a productive contact, and often less is more. They will appreciate your consideration of their time and busy schedule.

Make sure you have all the data pertinent to your phone call available. If you are calling to follow up on a quotation, make sure you have that quotation in front of you. Also, have a notebook or computer ready to take notes during the phone call. Usually there is so much information exchanged that you won't remember it all even if you think you will.

Write down any questions that require answers, so you don't forget them while you are on the call. One way to keep an eye on the ball is to keep crossing those notes off the list as you talk to make sure you have a good visual on the ones that are still unanswered. It does not show very good organization skills if you have to call again and again because you forgot to ask something.

## During the Call or Meeting

You have successfully set up a meeting or a call, and have your goal and questions all set. These will be your road map for the call. You have your computer on, and all the files related to the call are clearly in sight. At this point, it may be a good idea to silence your other phone and close your office door, or in the land of cubicles put up the *Do Not Disturb* sign. (You have one, right?) Getting interrupted right in the middle of your groove can ruin the dynamics of a call.

### Taking Notes

Keep good notes during the call. As mentioned above and bears repeating, there is always a lot of information that is exchanged, and you will not remember it all. There is also the chance that you will not know at the time if a piece of information is important or not. My rule: if it is coming from the customer, always assume it is somehow pertinent to your bid or the relationship.

The customer might say things like, "I just heard we are getting a new VP of Sales next month. The guy comes from xxx and his name is nnn." It may not seem related to your call right then, but it is important organizational information about your customer. The new VP's goals and objectives could very well affect you and your sales to the company. Perhaps the customer mentions that their maintenance department really likes ooo-company. They have been their exclusive supplier of these products for years. Or, he tells you that your price is good, but the competitor is the neighbor of the purchasing manager.

You can affect some of these circumstances, others you cannot. If you find yourself in a situation you cannot readily affect, like in the neighbor scenario above, you will need to find another way to market to this company. For example, find additional people within the company, beyond the purchasing manager, to help you apply pressure on the purchasing manager to give you a chance.

I have actually heard all of these things over the years, and every one led to the loss of a sale for me. If you are starting out, you may not put much value on these innocent sounding pieces of information, but they are hints that you may or may not get a sale. You have to take this into consideration when managing your time. That is why it is important to write down all information related to the customer, his organization, competitors, or just about anything else he talks about so you can review it later, and figure out its importance and relevance.

If you hear a new name related to your sale or product in general, you should immediately make a mental note to set up a meeting with that person to introduce yourself and your product. Every time a new person enters an organization, they bring with them their contacts, experience, and style. This could be good, indifferent, or terrible news for you.

## How is information presented to you?

Take notice of how details are presented to you because sometimes they hold clues to unspoken information.

Does your contact sound frustrated? This frustration could be directed at you, or it may not have anything at all to do with you. I have found that people who are leaning toward my direction sometimes get frustrated when other bidders gain a stronger foothold. My contact would like to tell me that I am wasting my time, but they can't, at least not directly and not now. The most they can do is drop hints (consciously or subconsciously). If you get a feeling that you are not being told all the information, it could mean you are not the front runner right now. On the flip side, if you call the customer to ask how their meeting with your competitor went, and he gives a little laugh and asks you what your calendar looks like the next week, it's a good sign. These are types of communication you can't get in an email, and you should make a note of them for your own records. Regardless of what someone else may claim, the phone is still the second best sales tool after a meeting. Period.

Keep in mind that if this customer is still talking to you, there are discussions, and they sound relaxed, it should be interpreted by you as good news.

Learning to read the signs will help you start recognizing when you will win an order, or if it's worth continuing to spend a lot of time and money on a quote.

## Asking for Clarification

If the success of the phone call or meeting goal is ambiguous, or you were unable to reach it, you should end the phone call or meeting with a clear question. "How do we proceed from here?" or "What's the next step?" Make a proposal, "How about I'll visit you next month," or something like that. This is the time to see how the meeting went. If it went well, the customer will give you some kind of indication. If not, you can read it in between the lines by the customer's vague responses or side stepping the issue.

> I once went to a meeting and at the end I asked, "Ok, how do we go from here?" The customer answered something like this, "We have your information, no need to call us. We will call you if we need you." Ok, how do you think my meeting went? Guess if I ever heard from them again. The worst part? I was at that meeting with my manager, and after we climbed into our rental car he announced, "That went really well. When do you think they will order from us?" I had to take a second look at him and ask, "Were we in the same meeting, or did we go to two different meetings? We will never hear from those guys." For those of you wondering – no, they never contacted us or responded to our calls.

See, after awhile even the biggest disappointments can turn into funny stories. The hard fact of sales is you *will* receive many no's. Not all meetings go well, and you'll lose orders. But, remember that one of the most important personality traits of top salespeople is they do not get discouraged (Chapter 3). Shake it off like a wet dog and move on to the next thing!

## After the Call or Meeting

After your call or meeting is over, you should finalize your notes in peace and quiet. Do yourself a big favor and do it as soon as possible. You are always left with an impression after a call or meeting, but as time goes by you will remember the meeting differently. Rethink the conversation and write down any pieces of information you did not have time to during the call. Who was on your side? Who wasn't? Include a paragraph about the feel of the communication, so you can track it as the sales process continues. This is especially useful if you are working on a bid that takes months because you will not remember all the small details and nuances later.

I usually write my notes at the airport on my way home from a meeting or at a local coffee shop right after the meeting if I'm driving. It gives me awhile to digest what happened, and it's still fresh enough to clearly remember everything. When I am back in my office, I compare these notes to previous ones. If I've had six phone calls and meetings with the customer about this proposal and they were all good, and this last meeting was also good, I can assume I am somewhere near the front of the pack of bidders. If all the other meetings were good and this one did not go so well, I have to assume that something has happened. Maybe I am no longer the lead candidate. If this is the case, it is important that I recognized it because I can start calling my contacts to find out what's going on and plan how to remedy it. The worst thing you can do is ignore it.

You must be truthful and as objective as possible when writing your notes. Otherwise, they are of no help at all. If, at the end of the year, you have had a total of 200 fantastic meetings that led to 45 good chance proposals with 30 customers, but received only 1 or 2 orders; then, maybe you are not being truthful to yourself or you have to work on your cue-reading skills.

Remember, these notes are for you. They are yours alone and meant to help you. I never gave any of these notes to my manager, and as a manager I never wanted to see any of my salespeople's notes either. I am not even sure anyone else ever did this. If you do decide to share yours, you run the risk of others misunderstanding you because everyone perceives situations differently. You need to find out how reliable you are in predicting your cases and see what works for you. By sharing your notes, you also run the risk of gearing your notes for a third party to see and losing the value of recording your gut reaction (intuition), which is what you were trying to accomplish in the first place.

It is a good habit to send a confirmation via email after a phone call. There are two reasons for this. One, the person sees that you are following up with them after the phone call. Two, in case there is a misunderstanding there is higher chance of it being cleared up quickly.

## First Impressions

Every time we have contact with a customer, we create and leave impressions. They can be based on anything from how we look, talk, and dress, to how deep our product knowledge or our sense of humor. Individual characteristics accumulate quickly, in as little as 15 seconds, and form a person's first impression of us. This impression can be transferred to reflect upon our product and company. Remember the old saying? You never get a second chance to create a first impression. Once it's done it's done, and you can't take it back. This works to our advantage if the first impression is positive, not so much if it is negative.

### Can I change a first impression?

Of course there is the possibility of changing someone's opinion of you, but it takes a long time and plenty of effort. Surprisingly, proving that a wrong impression is "wrong" is not the hard part. The hard part is getting a person to admit it to themselves. Humans do not like admitting to themselves that they are wrong. Instead, the tendency is to look for things that strengthen an opinion that is already created. This is one of the reasons we fight so enthusiastically against change, and why that first meeting is so important.

If the customer has a neutral opinion of you, they neither like you nor do they dislike you. It is much easier to convert that opinion to a positive one, rather than a negative opinion to even a neutral one.

Below is an opinion ruler:

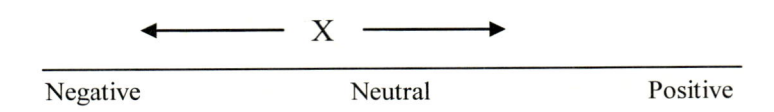

|  ←     X     →  |
|---|
| Negative     Neutral     Positive |

Since the first impression can fall anywhere on this ruler, it is worth investing in that first impression. Never underestimate the power of meeting with anyone for the first time.

Because people share their opinions with other people, someone may already have a disadvantage of being labeled long before the first meeting.

> We received a flyer advertising heating oil that, according to the correspondence, was significantly below the advertised price of other companies in the area. Since I was skeptical about how they could sell heating oil at that price, and am always interested in different selling styles, I called them. Jessica promptly answered my call. I explained why I was calling, and she told me she would pass me to William, their vice president of sales. I told William that I had received their flyer and was interested in ordering a couple hundred gallons of heating oil. He said that first, he would have to send a technician to inspect my furnace to make sure it was working properly; then, I would have to sign up for their furnace maintenance program for a minimum of one year. I told William that I had a good, working furnace that was recently serviced, and that I did not need that kind of service. "All I need is a couple hundred gallons of heating oil," I said. William got rip-roaring mad at me. "Well, if you're only looking at heating oil

why are you calling a full service heating oil company?" I paused a moment and answered, "Because you are a heating oil company selling heating oil?" He told me that they are not interested in customers who only look at price, and if I did not understand the value of their long history and their full service offering; then, the price for *me* was $x.xx per gallon, which was significantly above the market rate.

The entire phone call lasted less than five minutes. You can imagine what my impression of that "full service heating oil company" was, and still is. If William was not the owner's son, I suspect that he would have gotten the boot a long time ago. At least the other heating oil companies in the area must love William. Since I will most likely never call this company again, how can they change their first impression?

I know that there are many companies using the same sales and advertising strategy as the heating oil company in the example above: the *here is a low price and when you call there are expensive strings attached to the product* strategy. But, I'm not sure this style is really the best one. As far as William's outburst, I have a feeling that I was not the first person to call because of the low advertised price and end up an uneducated bargain shopper who did not understand their inherent value.

I would like to close this section with the following advice: it costs you nothing to be polite to people and create a good first impression. You never know who can help you down the road or what people are saying about you behind your back, and it's much better if it's positive rather than negative.

# PART III:
# QUOTATIONS & PRICING

# 6.

# WHAT TO OFFER AT WHAT PRICE

## Start With a Need to be Filled

One of the dangers of becoming an expert in a field is that we, as salespeople, start seeing what a customer needs; sometimes before the customer knows it themselves. So, why is this a problem? It's a problem because as the customer explains to you what they *think they need*, you actually see what they really need is something different. This may be the first time when the customer is buying this product or service, but it can be the hundredth time you are selling it and have gone through the same scenario with previous customers.

If the customer does a lot of work on the go and is convinced that they need a new smart phone, and you are convinced that they actually need a tablet, do you bring it up? The customer may get mad at you for interfering if you do because they have already determined what they need and it is their decision, not yours.

What if one employee of the customer was responsible for putting together the specification? If you call them, more or less to tell them in between the lines that they have specified their need incorrectly, they may not like hearing it. If you call their boss, they will hate you for sure for going over their head and discrediting them and their work. What if you offer what they asked for, and someone else tells them what you already knew, and the other company gets the sale because this customer actually appreciated the advice? What then? It looks like you were just trying to sell a product and not help the customer at all. The point being, it is not an easy situation.

Because I am in sales, I would definitely quote what the customer asked for. In addition, I would tell them that there may also be alternatives. Bring the subject up as food for thought and see if they are receptive to the idea. You are not criticizing what they have asked for; you are simply offering another option that may yield better results, or perhaps save them money. One way to do this is to say, "Lately there have been a lot of customers like you, but they ended up going with ... because of ... " This can be a good sales tool, especially when the customer saves money or becomes more efficient.

## Price Shock Theory

A silly way to lose an order is to not offer enough or to offer too much in your bid. If you offer too much, you may think that you are impressing the customer, but pretty much the only thing the customer will remember is your high price. This is especially true with large sales where it is impossible for the customer to fully inhale everything in your 86 page quotation. They turn to the price page first, and BAM! first impression created. If you don't offer enough, the customer may think that you don't have a suitable product or can't do it.

Personally, I drop out some of the options the customer asks for during the first phase of the quotation, and here is why: between the two options of not enough and too much, I'd rather offer not enough in order to present an attractive first price.

If you do not offer enough features, functions, or capabilities the customer will tell you, and because your price is attractive they will give you a chance to revise your offer. Most of the time the customer will remember the low price sticker, and you should still be in good shape. If you do the opposite and offer absolutely everything you can in your first proposal, the customer will inevitably think that you are expensive. This is the way we customers are. Then, when you start chipping features and options away, the customer will still remember that you were expensive and that you are now offering a less attractive version of the product. They will get the feeling that you first offered a good solution, and now you are offering them your second class product. Meanwhile, the competitor that held back on the first offer is getting the opposite psychological effect. The customer is convinced that they first offered the company's good product and now they are getting their best, premium one. Even if the customer recognizes that your new price is lower than your original price, it is a huge mental block to overcome. This is a concept many sales managers do not understand or even realize happens, but I suggest you remember it.

Again personally, I first offer a product or service that *just* meets the customer's requirements, maybe even slightly under. (Of course it has to be a working solution; I don't leave any material items out.) Then I tout the price. "See, dear customer, we worked really hard and we got you an awesome price."

Going back to your homework from previous chapters, you will need to know what your competition is offering and have a general idea of the customer's purchasing style. Do they buy the most expensive or the cheapest? The highest quality or best for the price? (Highest price doesn't necessarily mean the highest quality, but high priced sellers usually use quality as justification for their price.)

## Government Style Bidding

The reason I use my approach is because a lot of suppliers use a bidding style on their clients that I have coined as "government style" bidding. This style bidding implies that all required components and functions are included in the price, but when the project is executed the customer finds out that they were not, and are then, more or less, forced to keep adding new purchase orders to the existing one at hefty prices. The entire cost of a project usually ends up much more than the next cheapest bid that had all the components included. This is a very profitable way of doing business because those change orders and add-ons are pumped up with high profit margins.

No customer wants to admit when this happens because they would look like an idiot, and they are afraid of the ramifications to their job for – to put it bluntly – doing a horrible job evaluating vendor bids. Most likely, they comfort themselves by thinking that all other vendors would have done the same thing. So, they stay quiet, their boss stays quiet, and so on. And, quietly, they vow that next time they will do a better job evaluating bids. Customers that have gotten burned in the past by this style of bidding try to assemble minutely detailed specifications in order to prevent it from happening again. Even if I lose the current order based on this pricing style, I hope the next time the customer will be better educated about evaluating bids and making sure that all bidders have offered a complete package.

Whenever I bid on cases where the customer is, more or less, forced by their internal policy to buy from the lowest price bidder, a big part of my strategy is to educate the customer throughout the bidding process to make sure that all vendors have included the same things in their offer.

## Full Offer or Incremental Bidding

Incremental bidding is another popular method for keeping a customer's interest without overwhelming them. This is particularly common with large projects.

A quotation is first written with a broad stroke to get a dialogue started with the customer. The intention is not to answer every question, but to whet the appetite. As a project nears order, the quotation grows more detailed and larger as questions are answered and specifications are added. At this point, the quotation process itself is more labor intensive and costly.

A customer first calls a builder to ask how much a 4 bedroom; 3 bath; 3,000 sq ft house costs in his new development. The builder gives a price of $350,000-$450,000, depending on the materials and finishes. This is his first broad stroke quotation. The next quotation may have 3-6 pages, and more specifications about the project. The new price, based on those few pages of specifications, is narrowed to $385,000-$405,000. The process is repeated until the buyer has decided on the features they want, and are willing to pay for. The last quotation may be very detailed and have a fixed base price with some additional options, and specify how much each option costs and the timeframe for making a decision.

> Sales is a process, and you need to adjust your process speed to match the customer's speed. Inexperienced salespeople tend to get impatient and reveal all their cards too early in the game.
>
> ―
>
> Sales is often a battle of ideas – who can come up with the best solution to the customer's problem? If you give away all your best ideas too early, those ideas may be used to educate another bidder.

There are different sales strategies for quoting. One strategy is to price in a very low profit margin on the base deal and then add a much higher profit margin on change orders and add-ons throughout the project. This is similar to what happens in government style bidding, discussed in the previous section. Another alternative is to provide a full proposal on day one. As I explained above, this is not my preferred method of quoting. In addition to the price shock theory I put forth in the previous section, a customer may not be ready for a lot of detailed information yet. As the sales process progresses, the customer will be educated about the products and services being offered by you and your competitors. They will educate themselves, as well. Requirements will change. If you give a full blown proposal on day one, it is most likely that your quote will be used as the measuring stick and an educational tool. This may sound good to some people, but it does not sound good to me. Your competition may see or accidentally get a copy of your proposal, which obviously gives them a distinct advantage over you.

On the other hand, if you do not give enough information to keep the customer's interest in the process, you can lose a sale.

> A few years back, I quoted a project to a new customer. We had tried to become their supplier for years, and had quoted many times before, but never got an actual order. In the meantime, my company had developed a really nice feature for our equipment that significantly saved on operational costs. Due to our invention, we felt comfortable that this was the one! We were going to get this order.
>
> The customer had 12-15 people present at the final technical meeting. Their project manager told us that we needed to go over the special feature in detail, so everyone could understand it. We did. At the end of the presentation, I stepped right on a well-camouflaged land mine. The customer told us they now understood the details of our special feature; then, they asked, "Is this method patented?" I should have known better and seen what was coming. But I did not. I answered, "No, it is not, but it took us many attempts to get it right."

By now, you can guess the outcome. We lost the order, and the same company that we had lost the other orders to built exactly the same solution we had proposed.

If you think it still burns ... you are right! It does. The worst part is that with one lost sale, we lost that competitive technical edge against one of our major competitors.

Against common belief, if you make your first quotation too perfect, the customer has no reason to talk to you. All the answers are right in front of them in black and white. What you want to do instead is create a back and forth working relationship with the customer. The best way to achieve this is to give enough information in the quote to impress the customer; get them talking to you, but hold some information back to use later to keep their interest. Give them a reason to contact you with minor clarifications. Your goal is to keep the channels of communication open because every time you speak with a customer on the phone or meet with them in person, you learn a bit more about them, their need, and their style.

## Options

It is important to keep all additional, "nice to have" features as options. Remember, a required feature is a must have regardless of price. A desired feature is a feature one would like to have if there is enough money available.

My quotes always have a base price with options listed separately. Then, I keep repeating that base price because I want the customer to remember that the base price is affordable and competitive. After all, they don't have to buy all the options. Even when a customer asks you to include some of your options in the base price, you should consider twice before doing it. Trust me; the customer does have the ability to add numbers together. If your numbers are clearly shown as a base price and each separate option, the only thing you are doing by including options in the base is inflating your own base price. From that point on, the customer will remember the higher price and compare it to other companies' base prices. You will not benefit.

The request for options to be included into the base price is a good sign for you. The customer's team really liked the options you were offering and got excited about them. In some ways they are afraid that the project, due to additional cost, will not include these options. To avoid this, they ask you to bury them in the base price. This is the motivation behind the, "Let's include it in the base price." Be careful about how you keep that momentum working to your advantage. My advice is to make a separate section in the quotation somewhere between the base section and the rest of the options, and call it Preferred Options. I can't stress enough that combining them all into one line item can in no way work to your benefit. Sales professionals will still do it, though, because they want to report big numbers about their prospects. It is much nicer to report to their manager that they have a quotation out worth $6.2 million versus a quotation worth $4.1 million with $2.1 million in options because just like the customer your manager will remember $4.1 million, not $6.2 million. Just remember when the impulse to do this strikes, you are doing the exact opposite of what you need to show the customer to win a sale.

## Delivering Your Offer

There are many ways to deliver an offer to a customer. Often not much thought is given to what is the best way. However, the more expensive an item or service, the more thought should be given. I can't imagine a company purchasing a new production line receiving quotations by email only. They would have several meetings with potential suppliers to get to know them, and along the way measure and compare bidders to see who they feel they can trust.

These are the most common ways to deliver a bid:

- In person
- By email (call afterwards to make sure it arrived)
- Sending a paper copy via postal or letter service company (sometimes required)

- Verbally on the phone (send an email afterwards as confirmation)
- Sending a text message
- Filling out information directly on the customer's website request form

By far the best way to deliver a bid is in person, especially if you review the quote with the customer and are able to see their initial reaction. Remember, this is an important data collection tool to see where you stand in the game because even if someone wants to, initial reactions are difficult – if not, almost impossible – to fully hide. In every case, the more direct interaction you have with the customer, the better.

# 7.

# QUOTATION ANALYSIS

A typical salesperson is always busy. Rarely, is there slack time when there is absolutely nothing to do. It can feel like they are pushing a bicycle up the road because there's not enough time to stop, get on the bicycle, and start peddling – even if they know that if they took the time to get on the bike they would move much faster. This is one of the reasons why in depth quotation analysis is often ignored. There's always one more thing to get done, and then there will be time. Meanwhile, another emergency pops up.

Many salespeople believe spending the effort on analysis is a waste of time, more useless reporting to be done. They don't understand how, or believe it will help them. Unfortunately, this attitude represents a lack of comprehension of the overall sales process, and a fear of placing a measurable value on judgment. It also means that the person assigning a value must be able to back those numbers up with facts, not only opinions or wishes. It's easy to throw around opinions, but assigning an actual value incurs accountability. A simple way to begin this task is ranking open quotations in order from low chance to high chance of getting an order.

When I was starting out in my first job after graduation, I attended a company-wide meeting where the incoming CEO introduced himself. He was a Harvard graduate, and I was very impressed just based on the rumors floating around about him before I even saw him. During his presentation, he brought up something that in and of itself was not rocket science, but resonated with me. He told us that in business if you start measuring something, anything really, the values will go up. Not necessarily because we are getting better at it, but just because we are measuring it. It is the natural tendency of people to do that part well which they know is being measured. I have thought about this a lot, and he was absolutely right. It is not the measuring effort itself that will improve the subject matter. It is people knowing that something is measured that will make them automatically try to be better, faster, cheaper, etc.

Now since we know this, let's use it to our advantage.

## What to Quote

Marketing people tell us that in order to sell we must solve a customer's problem. That is a fine idea, but how do we know what is the customer's problem?

> A customer sends you a quote request asking for 100 pieces of standard 8" flat edge shovels. Is someone really going to call the customer and ask them what they are trying to move, or why they need so many shovels? Will they ask them if they've considered a backhoe instead? The quote request already specifies the customer's problem. He needs 100 shovels.

Sometimes the customer's problem is so obvious it requires no further thinking or analysis. It is important to know this because it is also human nature to quote what we think will best suit the customer's need *as we perceive it*.

If our product offering includes only one kind of 8" flat edge shovels, choosing a product to offer is easy. The problem arises when we have 12 different shovels from 4 different manufacturers that all fit the general description. Now, as the salesperson, your job is to assess which one of those shovels this customer would be most likely to buy because it is not your job to just send out quotations, it is your job to send out quotations leading to profitable orders.

Flexibility to analyze items to be included in a quotation will depend on the customer's specification. The more detailed the specification, the tighter the guidelines are when choosing a product from your portfolio. A customer may want a quote for a specific manufacturer and model number, and in those cases you should respond with that particular item. (Competition is more transparent when the same manufacturer and model are required.)

Other times the customer will allow you to quote a comparable product by another manufacturer as an alternative, and you will make your decision based on the following criteria:

- You think, or even know, that you are getting more competitive pricing from an alternative supplier, which betters your chances of getting the order based on price
- You believe that the product is genuinely better than the one the customer asked for, which betters your chances of getting the order based on quality or technical advantage
- You are limited by your product portfolio and an item is all you can offer, so you are hoping that your service skills and the customer's trust in you will get you the sale

Even when a supplier has leeway to choose a different product to fulfill a customer's need, it is sometimes better to choose one that is expected because the customer may be afraid of a generic version. This is especially true if the product is a direct replacement spare part or an added feature on an existing proprietary system.

If a quote request is a generic one and there are several different alternatives that could fulfill the application; then, the supplier should speak with the customer and clarify what they want and what features they appreciate.

Going back to the shovel example, it would be silly to send out twelve offers or one offer with twelve different alternatives. The sensible thing to do is to call and explain the alternatives, the differences between them, and the cost impact of each feature. Three things will happen:

- You talk to the customer and get a chance to create a relationship
- You narrow down the features and price level that the customer expects
- You gain the trust and likeability of the customer by getting their feedback about what exactly to offer

A customer's decision is rarely based on a single feature or value, but rather on a combination of features; a package. You must always be able to justify why you are quoting what you are quoting.

Again, let's revisit the above shovel example.

You call the customer and you find out why they need the shovels. After learning the application, you know based on your prior dealings with other customers that a 6" shovel is perfect for this job. Find out if the customer knows about the 6" shovel in your portfolio and introduce them to this product. Tell them, in detail, about the other projects you worked on. If the customer gives you a green light to offer that as an alternative, there is a very good chance you will get the order.

## Setting Prices

The three most important reasons why people buy what they buy and where they buy: price, price, and price. This doesn't necessarily mean customers only buy the lowest price. It's not the absolute price that counts; it's the perceived value compared to the price that is important.

Customers do not mind paying more if they feel they are getting a better deal with the pricier alternative.

Bidders need to be well priced against competitors for comparable products. A customer may buy an expensive sports car – more expensive than she originally planned – because she got an "awesome price." Another customer may purchase something because "it was on sale."

Before we get into the reasons why people choose price over value, let's look at price formulation. Whether you are working for a manufacturer or reseller, you always have to deal with pricing. Very few companies have a set price that will always be the same, regardless of the circumstances. On the contrary, there are several, sometimes dozens, or even hundreds of pricing schemes depending on the market, the territory, and the customer. Sometimes I truly wonder how companies can keep tabs on all these pricing schemes for the same product, but what I really wonder is how those customers that are paying higher prices than others would feel if they found out.

One of the reasons why companies like Walmart are so successful is because of their huge purchasing power. They are able to set lower prices on selected items at their stores because they do not pay as much for products from the manufacturer as smaller outfits do. By the same token, it's worth for a manufacturer to sell to Walmart with lesser profit because they sell large volumes. In the bargain they gain brand recognition and market penetration, but limit their ability to increase profit margins.

Profit margins, obviously, are an important part of building your quotation. Every company has their own view on the power of individual salespeople to set profit margins:

- A company allows the sales force to set margins within established limits. These limits can be liquid or set in stone.

- A company sets the profit margin or sales price, and the sales force has no control over pricing or margins. Grocery stores are a good example. The price is what it is, and you know that at the time when you put an item in your cart.
- A company allows a fixed sales price, and the sales force is not privy to information like product cost or profit.

In the typical B2B environment, due to higher overall profit margins there is no real set pricing. A company may have a sales guide that states they are looking for a certain amount in profit margin, either in absolute currency or in percentage of sales; for example, 20%. Naturally, the margin varies depending on what the company counts into cost and how the margin is expressed. In this case, each sales manager is given a goal of 20% margin on their quotations. However, depending on the actual situation, the margin could be 5% or it could be 40%. Most companies track salespeople by total sales and margin created.

Regardless of the margin used, a salesperson should be able to justify the reason they used it. For example, if a customer expresses an expectation for a shovel to cost $80/piece, and a salesperson can sell them shovels for $79 with a 16% margin; most salespeople will likely do it. Why keep a 20% margin and take the chance of losing the order over a few bucks?

If a customer is a loyal repeat customer, it is possible they may not feel too badly paying a little more to purchase from you. Sending out a bid of $84/shovel could still lead to an order as long as the customer doesn't feel that you are gouging them.

## Who Are the Other Bidders?

You must know who you are competing against. Without this knowledge you can easily be blindsided during the sales process.

There are always competitors you don't mind going up against and those you do. No matter how you feel, one of the worst things you can do is underestimate your competitor. They are a working company with a viable product or service, and they are just as hungry as you are to get orders. Never forget it.

Learning about your competitors and their products will also teach you about your customers. Some will favor you, but others will tend to prefer your competitor. It will be up to you to find out why these customers want to do business with your rivals, so you can break the cycle and win them over.

> A trucking company owns 35 Volvo trucks. Due to a lack of resources, the maintenance department is continuously working overtime to keep the fleet in good and safe condition. The maintenance supervisor may lean heavily on the project team to persuade them to acquire only Volvos. His reasoning is that the mechanics already know how to service Volvo trucks and won't require additional training. They also keep an inventory of spare parts for Volvos. Buying a new brand means buying and stocking additional spare parts. Thus, if you were selling another brand and your price, the delivery time, and even financing may have been better, you still lost the order because the "whisperer" of the maintenance department unofficially decided the outcome by leaning on the perceived decision makers. (I talk more about whisperers in Chapter 12.)

In every company each of the separate disciplines (maintenance, engineering, IT) has a varying amount of "leaning power." During the sales cycle, you need to keep your antenna up to find out which discipline(s) can't be against you in order for you to win the sale. If you find out early enough, you can still do something about it. If you find it out as a reason for having already lost a bid, it is too late.

As the salesperson for this case, it would also be useful to know if the company has more than one brand of trucks. If you walk into their yard and you only see Volvo's, this is not going to be an easy sale.

You will not know what to do to make it better unless you know your weak spots in the customer's eyes, or in their evaluation process. Even if a discipline is against you, you may survive. Be aware, though, that some are outright lethal, and you can't recover regardless how much people wanted your product. In the case of the trucks above, perhaps you can offer a maintenance and on-site spare parts package for your truck make at a reduced rate for the first three years.

If you lose the truck order, you may think there were some shady dealings going on. Well maybe, but statistically it is very unlikely. The fact is you should have recognized the issue and come up with a solution. Period.

Periodically analyzing your weak points and strong points and comparing them against your competitors is important. Do not fall into a lull where months and years go by, and you are still working off the same intelligence or information.

Your success rate will be higher (and your life easier) when you compete against your preferred competitors, the ones that are weaker than you are. However, you can't take it for granted that you will always win, and concentrate all your time trying to beat your fiercest competitors. You need to defend your turf against those competitors you usually win against, as well. To them, you are the fiercest competitor.

## Increase Your Chances of Getting an Order

The sales professional should always be evaluating, internally qualifying, and re-qualifying prospects and quotations they are working on. To the untrained eye it seems unnecessary, but it is an effective way to make sure you are spending your time in the right places. This means spending your time on customers and quotations that are most likely to turn to orders. In this chapter, I will teach you how to evaluate your quotations and decide which ones should receive the bulk of your resources because for the salesperson, one of the worst things is committing time and energy to a project that will never be won.

You are probably wondering why a salesperson would keep working a *dead horse* quote, that project that will never be won, but it happens more often than you think. The first issue is to identify the dead horse, which can be difficult. When a quotation is discussed during an internal sales meeting, it is examined through rose colored glasses. The salesperson desperately wants the order, and the sales director needs the order to make budget. Everyone gets excited, and the general opinion is that this sale will happen. No one wants to be the negative jerk to throw a cold bucket of reality on all these good feelings as the bearer of bad news. Instead of examining the facts of the situation, advice such as, "Tell the customer this … and tell them that … ," or "Call the customer right now," or "Call them again," gets thrown around the table as a solution to landing the order. The real problem is that people are wishing and hoping more than collecting intelligence, objectively analyzing it, remedying the situation, and giving solid advice. Internal hopes and dreams are not enough to get a customer to buy from you. Otherwise, sales meetings could easily be converted to events where everyone sings "Kumbaya" and tells each other how they definitely hope they get this next big order.

Every salesperson needs an evaluation system that is based on facts. It needs to recognize the strong points of the product or service you are offering as well as the weak points to improve the chances of getting an order. While improving upon weak points, one has to concurrently build upon the strong points too.

Every company has a competitive edge; something they do better than the competition. Otherwise, they don't stay alive for long. A good sales strategy is to steer the customer's focus to your competitive edge and away from the competitor's strong points. (Just keep in mind that the other guys are trying to do the same thing.)

Each sales win or loss should be carefully assessed to find the reasons why an order was received or lost. Both cases are equally important. This is the time for an honest evaluation, not a finger pointing session to assign blame. The purpose is to determine where a bid went right or wrong, so that strengths can be built upon and mistakes can be prevented next time. In the end, when handled correctly both the salesperson and the entire sales department can benefit from these.

Earlier, you were asked to compile a list of competitor strengths and weaknesses along with the reasons a customer does or does not buy from you. You will need that information to build your evaluation system.

## Create an Evaluation System

Make a list of the top 5 values that are important to your customer when choosing a supplier. These can include things that the customer has directly told you, indirectly told you, or ones you assume that they appreciate or value the most. Is it the price, technology, the color? Maybe it's the fact that a product is made in America. Keep in mind that these values might surprise you, and that assumed values do not hold the same weight factor as those provided by the customer. If you are working on a sizable order, why not ask the customer straight out what are the five most important values that vendor selection will be based on? If you ask, there is a chance they will tell you. You don't have to ask for all five at the same time. You can ask leading questions, "I assume that yyy is more important to your organization than zzz." Then, you can ask if you are assuming right. Let them correct you, revealing the information you were after in the first place.

Next, make another list of your top competitors and include your own company name. Using the information you gathered about each competitor, assign a rating to each company (including yours) based on the customer values above. The best will receive 10 points, second best 8 points, third best 6 points, fourth best 3 points, and the worst one gets a 0. Be honest.

When you tally up the points for each company, some pertinent information becomes clear:

- Where you stand on the list
- Which areas are your weak areas; they will need attention
- Is it worth your time to continue bidding on this particular job?

In order to be first on the list you do not need all 10's. You just need to avoid the 3's and the 0's. A good, solid product can have 6's and 8's in the mix, and still come ahead of the competition.

If you are dead last of the five bidders, or even fourth, you have to ask yourself: if you were the customer, would you buy from you? If the answer is no or probably not, you have a few options. If you aren't working on any other pressing quotes, you can continue the process with a modified goal of developing the customer relationship versus the goal of winning the order. However, you also have to remember that if your product is not as good as others, you may leave a lasting impression with this customer that your product will always be *not as good* as an alternative, so this strategy could backfire on you. If it is a question of price, there is less chance of this happening, but if it is a question of technology or performance, you will want to think this through.

The same is true if your price is much higher; the customer might think you are always going to be pricey. It may not be worth quoting products that are clearly not your strongest offerings to a new customer, or where you really do not understand the product or application. In a case like this, it could actually be better to tell the customer that you do not have the capacity to quote at this time, but that you would be more than happy to keep receiving their requests and maybe next time you will have the time to serve them the way they deserve. Existing long time customers are much more forgiving when it comes to a favored supplier not being the best of the pack. Whatever you decide to do, just be careful and make sure you are fully aware of the potential consequences. Unless you are a business owner, make sure you have organizational approval for your action beforehand.

# 8.

# PRICING AND PRICE ELASTICITY

If we are to believe the advertisements on television or the flyers inundating our mailboxes, price, price, and price are the three most important reasons why people buy what they buy and where they buy. The best part is it looks like absolutely *everyone* has the best price. How is that possible?

If price is really that important when we are buying for personal reasons, what happens when we, as individuals, travel from home to work and make purchasing decisions for our job? Do we behave the same way we do at home? Experience tells me the answer is yes and no. I wanted to make this comparison to remind you that *people*, not companies, make the purchasing decisions for your customer.

Admittedly, price is very important, but it is definitely not the only determining factor in a purchasing decision. Depending on the product and industry, there is much more at play than price alone. There is customer service, spare parts, maintenance, perceived knowledge of personnel, company, and product reputation to name a few.

If someone is in the market to purchase a new washer and dryer, they have many alternatives to choose from. A mere ten minutes on the internet searching for prices, and they will have a pretty good idea of the market price of a washer/dryer, model numbers, and specifications as well as quality reviews by other customers. Within those ten minutes, the customer has also, more or less, found the price and quality point they are willing to buy at. Every customer formulates their own market price, and it can vary significantly from one customer to another.

## Project Budgets

Once a customer compiles a budgetary quotation from market data, they typically add their costs and some contingencies (I have seen anywhere from ±10% to ±25% used), and this number becomes their first estimate of how much a project can cost. It is to your benefit to find out what this budget is based on. Which company did they use to determine market pricing? If it was yours; then, you already know the number, which is great. If it was another company, try to find out which one.

Once you know who they are it should be quite simple to estimate how they compare technically and cost-wise to your product offering. Another good reason to attempt leading the customer's budgetary quotation is the possibility of introducing your ideas and solutions to the customer's personnel long before a project is even approved. This technique, sometimes know as consultative selling, is underutilized by many companies in sales today. The one doing the consultative selling always has the best chance of getting the purchase order. It's why some companies *are* doing it. Often a project is consulted and quietly purchased without the competitors even hearing about it until after the fact. These deals usually have a sweet profit margin, as well.

## Quoting to Stay in the Game

There can be too many companies bidding on a project for the customer to spend time with all of them. In these cases, it is common for the customer to carry out a first cut of the least favorite bidders. It may be based on the initial budgetary price provided by the bidders, or simply based on references and perceived capability. At this point, it could be detrimental if you deliver the wrong type of proposal. Some common reasons why a bidder is cut:

- The quotation included too many options, driving the price higher, and the customer thought it was too expensive.( The customer did not do a thorough comparison yet; they just took a quick look at them.)
- The quotation did not include enough of the features the customer asked for, and they concluded that the bidder doesn't have the capability to fulfill their requirements.
- The bidder failed to demonstrate similar references.
- The customer does not believe that the bidder can meet the required delivery time.
- The bidding company is relatively young, and the customer is afraid that it won't be around in the future to support them.

Find out the basic assumptions the customer will use, or used, to establish their financial budget early on so you can quote accordingly. After the customer receives the first 5-7 bids, they typically drop the most expensive bid. Even if the supplier had great products for the project they may never get a chance to present them. The basic thinking is that they had the same chance as everyone else did to submit a solid first bid.

## Discounts

As discussed in previous chapters, offering an early discount can hurt you. In my opinion, it is much better to present a consistently good and competitive price throughout the sales process versus keeping a higher price throughout the process, with the thinking of giving a big discount at the end. Otherwise, you may be eliminated from the bidding race long before the opportunity to give those discounts ever arises. I would however, depending on the project being quoted, save room for a small discount. Even if it is priced into the quote, it still leaves a good impression with the buyer. After all, the buyer needs to justify their existence to their organization. If they never get any discounts, folks may start thinking they are not doing their job very well.

Having said this, there are kamikaze type companies where the strongest, perhaps only, sales strategy is to drop the price as low as it takes to get the job; then, worry about how to execute the project later. I have heard such claims as, "Our company's strategy is to take the order first. Once we take the profit out, that shows how much money we have left to fulfill the contract." As a customer, how would you feel hearing that? Would you think you are getting a quality product?

Competing with these companies based on price alone is almost impossible because their goal is not to make a profitable sale at the time of the sale, but to gain customers. They either milk those customers after they have signed on the dotted line or recoup the discount from the project. Neither outcome is desired by the customer. All you can do is set the customer's expectation for quality and deliverables at such a high level that these companies are continuously losing money, and are driven out of the marketplace. Many purchasing teams drop the lowest bidder, as well, in the first round of cuts for this reason. Especially if the price is significantly lower than the others. Unless the supplier has a very good explanation for their price level, the purchasing team suspects they are conducting business like the company mentioned in the previous paragraph, and they aren't willing to take on that fight.

## Pricing Strategies

If you are selling the only product or service within your category and market segment, you are able to include healthier profits in your price as compared to being in a marketplace for commodities where competition is abundant. Basically, the less differentiating features between your product and that of your competitor, the more price comparison will affect your sales.

> If you are a farmer growing Russet potatoes, you will have a tough time showing the difference between your

potatoes and the neighboring farmer's Russet potatoes, no matter how good a baked potato yours makes.

Formulating your price is important, so how is it done?

- Total cost is calculated; then, profit is added, including the profit for the representative if you are using one, and this gives you your list price. After the anticipated discount is subtracted from the total, the number becomes the final selling price.

- Tally up the cost; then, price the item per market conditions and see what is left in between for profit. This is why market positioning is so important. Choosing one or another segment can greatly affect selling price and consequently profits.

  In order to do this you need to know your competition well, so that when you are formulating a market price for your product you are sure you are comparing them feature to feature. A product's price is based on perceived value to the customer. If that value is higher than other products in the market, it can command a higher price and profit.

- The company adopts an assertive plan of temporarily slashing profits, or even selling at a loss to increase market share. The goal is to build future gains by creating name recognition and becoming a market leader. One of the large online bookstores is a good real life example of this practice.

  Grocery stores and big box stores use this strategy to drive in customers. A grocer may price milk at below cost knowing that rarely do customers come into the store and buy just milk. They usually buy other items, as well. Most customers know the approximate market price of milk and understand if the price advertised in the weekly flyer is a good deal. The grocery store also understands that even if they are losing a few cents per carton, the company will not suffer significant losses; especially, if other product sales increase as a result of the milk pricing strategy.

Equipment manufacturers do this, as well. They may price a popular item at cost, or even at a loss to encourage supplemental business, such as spare parts or service. A few years ago, I was reading an annual report for a very large and reputable company. Within the small print there was an interesting statement that read like this, "For fiscal year xxxx, service and spare parts generated 128% of company profits." Doesn't that mean that the company is actually selling product at a loss?

It's very tough to fight against these tactics when you are expected to sell a product at profit from the very first unit. I've heard salespeople get advice like, "Just convince the customer of your product's value, and they will pay more," or "tell them our company is over 100 years old." But the fact of the matter is if there is no additional value to convince customers; then what? Sometimes it's worth concentrating your efforts elsewhere.

> Drive by a few car service shops and you are likely to see a sign by the side of the road advertising an oil change for only $19.95! What can't be read on that sign is that by the time a customer drives out of the parking lot that oil change will cost $35-$80. The $19.95 is a marketing tool to get customers in the door. Why does it work? The people who walk into the business are most likely in a need of an oil change, and once they are in the door they are less likely to drive off without placing an order even if the price is *slightly* higher than advertised.

This sales strategy can be rather dangerous because it may make customers upset when they realize they were pretty much duped into coming in.

- If you are the smaller, not as well known, perhaps not local competitor with no great technical advantages, you will probably need to be a lot less expensive than the big name player in the industry. In my experience, a price of 5% less is not enough to convince a customer to consider you, but at 20% less the customer simply cannot ignore you. You still may not get the order, but at least you will most likely be given a chance. This is why market newcomers often have to lower their price significantly below that of the established providers.

The classic sales style of industry leaders is highly psychological. They drop hints of failure if the customer buys from the wrong source. They press the belief that no buyer has ever been fired over buying from "Biggest Supplier Company." Earlier, I discussed the reasons why a customer buys from a large, established company. However, being a big company also has its downfalls. Big companies have higher overhead, meaning higher fixed costs. Even if they can acquire their product cheaper than you can, they also have more internal expenses. You can use that to your advantage when pricing a project. Inertia is also a common problem in large organizations.

- Lastly, a company can use an aggressive pricing strategy aimed not at winning an order, but at sinking profits for the competition. If a customer has chosen to buy from another supplier, sometimes the losing bidders send out one final quotation with a razor thin profit margin or no profit margin at all. The intent is to try and make the customer push the chosen supplier – the competition – to lower their price to the same level. If you exercise this option, keep in mind that it is still a legal proposal, and the customer may just surprise you and place an order to you instead.

## Turning the Discussion to Value

Customers like to focus discussions on price because it is so easy, tangible, and important. Sometimes it feels like it is the only discussion they want to have. Instead of arguing about price, it is better to divert the customer's attention by talking about the different features your product offers. Find out which options the customer really likes, and which ones they would be willing to drop in order to get the price lower. Make sure the customer realizes that the added features have an impact on the price. Price is always a trade-off between cost and content. Reducing content leads to a lower price, increasing content leads to a higher price.

Always have five significant points about your product or service that you know inside out, and try to steer the conversation to these points. There have been many times when an unsure customer has asked me to tell them why, exactly, they should buy from me. You have to be ready to discuss these points at all times, even if at the time it may sound like the customer is just taunting you. The fact is now you are talking about something other than price, and that is value.

Discussing value is positive while discussing price tends to be a negative conversation. Try to dominate discussions with the positive versus the negative.

## Product Price Comparison

One seasoned salesperson once told me, "Never underestimate how little the customer knows."

> We had just come from a customer visit where we saw a product the customer had purchased from our competitor

some time before. We had bid on the same project, but lost it. We were told that we were too expensive. After seeing the competitor's product, we realized that it was nothing like what we had offered, and there was no doubt that we were too expensive. As much as we hated to admit it, we realized that while we thought we had done a good job explaining our product and its features to the customer; we had failed. We talked about where we went wrong, and the only explanation we could find was that we should have explained everything about our offering from bottom up; slow and steady, steady and slow. We made too many assumptions that the customer knew more than they did. Our offer was technically way too advanced (meaning costly) compared to what the customer was willing to accept as a solution. It was in no way the customer's fault. It was our fault; our mistake.

I now tell salespeople that it never hurts to start at the beginning when explaining their product or service. Of course, there's a danger of boring those individuals who are already knowledgeable. When it is obvious that the customer knows what you are talking about, you can go through material at a faster pace. Also, bring up the information you feel is the most important multiple times from a different point of view. (Just like I do in this book.) This way, someone who did not get it the first time may get it the second time, and if they got it the first time, it is reinforced the second time. Even if you ask if there are any questions and no one speaks up, it doesn't mean everyone understood what you were talking about or fully got it. When you are presenting to a group of people, no one, and I mean absolutely no one, will admit that they did not understand what was said, especially if everyone else seems to have gotten it. For this reason, you have to ask smartly crafted questions like, "Should I go into more detail about … " or "Do you see this fitting your need?" or "Are there any features I haven't adequately covered yet?"

## Features and Options

Choosing what features to include in a quotation is a skill that a salesperson develops over time. There are many different schools of thought on the subject:

- Keep the offer very basic in order to attract the customer with a low price.
- Include all the nice-to-have options as separate line items in the quotation and let the customer choose what they want.
- Choose options for the customer based on past experience; the options the salesperson knows most customers want.

After working with enough customers, a salesperson will have statistics on their side and will learn what sells and what does not. For example, if you speak with a buyer at a good sized car dealership, they will be able to pinpoint the options most customers in their area want and are willing to pay for. They are the ones ordering the cars for the dealer's inventory, and because they order hundreds of them they have a very good idea of what customers want.

As I have already stated many times, my opinion is to keep the base offer low and present options with separate pricing. This does not mean offering a product that does not work unless the customer buys the extra options. The base price must include a functioning product or service. If you offer a customer a truck with no wheels in order to keep the base price low, knowing full well that they will need to buy wheels before they can drive the truck off the lot, it's doubtful the good feeling that went with the low price will continue after the customer realizes what you did.

## Moving to an All Inclusive Price

Keep product options separate in the quotation as long as possible to leave yourself wiggle room should it be needed to meet the customer's budget.

> Company LMNOP is quoting a complete package of furniture for a new 4 bedroom house. The package costs $79,900. Due to budgetary constraints ($68,000), the customer wants a $12,000 (15%) discount, which is not possible. However, at the same time they are adamant that they need every piece of furniture, and the only solution they see to make a deal is a significant price reduction or discount. Instead of jeopardizing the entire sale by just saying *No, can't do it*, the salesperson can explain that with the current pricing the discount is not possible, but if the customer changes the dining room table to another one, takes out the coffee tables, and swaps the couch the price can be reduced to $71,300, which is about 11% less than the original price, and so forth.

A salesperson should always give alternatives by starting with the word *yes* combined with *if*, "Yes, it is possible if we do ... " instead of, "No, it is not possible." *No* is a negative word and *yes* is a positive word. Never be negative.

After the customer has chosen the options they want included in a quotation, indicated it is within their budget, and are placing the order, it's time to move from the Base Price+Options (BPO) bid to a bid that includes an all inclusive final price. The BPO has served its purpose. You offered a product at a price that caught the customer's attention, and you are still in the race. Going into final negotiations, you will want the freedom of including discounts and profits anywhere in the pricing without it being obvious to the customer. Every company needs to make money to survive, but it is not to your benefit for the customer to know where you have profit and how much. Sometimes inexperienced or unsure salespeople are embarrassed by profits; don't be. Regardless of what the customer will tell you, they understand that you and your company must make a profit to pay the bills.

Confirm with the customer that it is understood what the options are, and in the case of competition that all bidders have the same options included in their bid, before submitting the final lump sum quotation. You want the customer to confirm that the scopes are comparable. This is a good time to ask a few questions to make sure. (Keep in mind it is entirely possible that they are only talking to you.)

A seasoned buyer will want to keep all options priced individually, so they can negotiate the price of each item separately. This negotiating style is lethal to your profits.

For example, if you have a product with an installation cost of $875, the customer may point out that another company is only charging $325 for installation. They may even cover the company name on a competitor's bid and show you the line item to prove it. Of course, the buyer will only point out items where you are more expensive in an attempt to get you to lower those prices. He will never show you the ones where you are cheaper. One way to counter this is to ask the customer to look at all option pricing and tell you where you are more expensive and where you are less expensive; then, add all the options together into a lump sum price and look at the total package. How does that package compare? If it is only the installation that costs more, perhaps you have a good reason why it is more expensive. If so, this is the opportunity to bring it up.

## The Sweetness of a Low Price

There is a good adage that says *the sweetness of a low price is well outlasted by the bitterness of a bad product.* My version is that you can't get a good and cheap product without buying two products: the good one and the cheap one. This is important for both the customer and the seller to understand. I have never had the *pleasure* of selling the least expensive product on the market. In fact, I have always been at the opposite end of the price curve, and have always had to convince the customer why they benefit by paying more.

The fact is that no matter how good your product is, if the price difference between it and the cheap version is too much, buyers are more likely to try the cheap one first. This struggle permeates everyday existence in both personal lives and in business lives.

No company selling the cheapest product will ever advertise like this, "This product is a piece of junk, but look at the price!" They are more likely to taunt you with, "Why spend your hard earned dollars on a new ... at ... when you can get one here for less than half price." Even seasoned buyers fall into this trap every single day.

> A few years ago, I dropped my cordless drill from scaffolding and cracked the case beyond repair. I needed a new one quickly. I knew I wanted a powerful one, and one that wouldn't need charging every 15 minutes. At the store I found a beautiful, big brand, yellow drill for $249. I thought it was pretty expensive, so I went to a discount store. There, I found another drill that looked like the first one for $49. I knew that the first drill was a good one because people who owned the same drill had told me they were happy with it. I had never heard of the other one.
>
> In order to justify buying the cheaper one, I told myself that I could buy FIVE cheap ones, including TEN batteries, for the price of the brand name drill with two

batteries. Was I just paying for a name and logo? And, even if I tried the cheap one first, I'd only lose $50. They were both made in the same country…

So, I bought the cheap one. And, it was junk. The batteries lasted for about 15-20 minutes, and the charger was slow. In a few weeks the spindle wore out and started wobbling. In the end, I bought the good one, and I still have it. The entire exercise ended up costing me $300.

The ironic thing is that I, who all of my working life have tried to convince customers to buy the good one, fell into the same trap as everyone else.

Since that incident, I now own a yellow name-brand circular saw, table saw, and nail gun. When I need new tools, I will pay significantly more to buy the same brand because I am convinced it will not let me down. I have become a brand loyal customer. As long as the company keeps producing a good product, I will keep buying. I have become a low transaction cost customer.

Naturally, the tables are turned if you are selling the cheaper drill. Then, the selling strategy is largely based on price. "It's only $50."

I have always said that my best potential customers are the ones who have already purchased "the cheap one" because they understand that there are other factors besides price to consider in a purchasing decision. If you are the one selling the expensive product, make sure you explain this to your customer.

# PART IV:
# TRACKING & ORGANIZATION

# 9.

# TRACKING QUOTATIONS

Every bid you or your company makes is an opportunity; therefore, each quotation needs a follow up. This means every sales professional must track their quotations. As said before, the goal of the salesperson is not only to make quotations; the goal is to make quotations that lead to good and profitable orders.

> I once spoke with the owner of a car body shop and painting business. He kept a long list of open customer quotes in a file on his computer system that was accessible to all his counter employees. When they had a few minutes of idle time in between customers, they picked up the phone and called the next potential customer on the list to follow up on a quotation. After the phone call, they either removed the quotation from the list as sold/lost/not proceeding or they dropped it to the bottom of the list where it worked its way to the top of the list again in few weeks time. Counter employees received a small bonus on the sales they made. This was a brilliant way to utilize employees' down time and follow up on quotations.

A large amount of sales cost and trouble is spent putting together a quotation. If the salesperson doesn't follow up, all that time and money is wasted. As long as a customer hasn't made a decision, there's still a chance to win an order. The fact that the customer has not yet ordered does not mean anything. It is not an indicator that they will not order at all. Always follow up until there is a confirmation of either a win or a loss.

Regardless of what your system is, you need to do your best to make sure nothing falls through the cracks. Tracking your quotations ensures that you respond to customers in a timely manner, and that you are taking the initiative and contacting the customer. If you track your quotations and follow through, it is guaranteed you will get better results. It is quite obvious, but I will say it anyway: it is a lot easier to get an order from your quotation backlog than from cold calling potential customers, so don't blow it by being lazy.

## The Top 5-Next 5 Concept

Since I started working in sales, I've pretty much had more work than time to finish it. Sometimes I wonder what it would be like to go to work knowing that I didn't have that much to do for that day, week, or month. This is another thing that I have noticed is common with all salespeople considered successful.

When you have more work load than you can handle, inevitably things start falling through the cracks, regardless how hard you try to prevent it from happening. You see every prospect as a potential customer, and enthusiastically promise to do something for everyone with every intention of actually doing it; then, something urgent springs out of nowhere. The job is a constant juggling of time. This may sound like a good thing, but it is not. What happens to customers that always get put aside; get their quotations late; don't get their quotations followed; or who would like you to visit them, but you don't have the time? They don't wait for you. They move on to other suppliers. To make it worse, when they talk to other prospects about your company, they are not exactly singing your praises. As a salesperson you do the best you can, but it's not always best for you or your company. So how do you work within these parameters?

Time is your most valuable resource. You have to make sure you are spending it wisely on prospects and potential projects that are most likely to yield the best results.

More often than not, this means you end up spending the majority of your time working with the same few customers. The more you work with them, the more they get to know you, and the more orders you receive from them. Since you get orders you like working with them, and voilà! A positive squirrel cage is up and running.

A long time ago, I developed my Top 5-Next 5 method to help me prioritize my time. It has helped me tremendously because it's simple to put into practice, and it works. I list my top 5 quotes on a piece of paper, usually a yellow post it note, and stick it at the upper right hand corner of my computer screen (very technical). This list has nothing but the names and quotation numbers of my most important quotes. I am looking for a highly visual reminder. I post another sticky note with my Next 5 at the bottom of the screen.

Every morning I look at my Top 5 list and make sure that any and all work required for each of these quotes gets done first. Nothing else matters until all the needs of the Top 5 are satisfied. Absolutely everything else comes second. Once I am done with the Top 5, I review the Next 5 list and see if those quotes need anything. Once the items necessary for Next 5 are done, I move on to my other quotations. It is important to keep the Next 5 list as accurate as possible too because as the Top 5 quotes are either landed as orders or lost, they will be replaced by quotes from the Next 5 list.

I decide which quotes to include on my Top 5 and Next 5 lists using the following criteria:

- When a decision will be made. The sooner the customer will decide, the higher they are on the list.

- The size of a potential order. The bigger the order, the higher it goes on the list.
- Which quotes I have the best chance of getting. A customer who has already ordered from me will be higher on the list than a new customer.
- Potential margin. If I have 2 quotes, $30k each, and one has a 12% margin and the other has a 21% margin, the quote with the higher margin will be higher on the list than the other one.

If you have two conflicting parameters; for example, a high margin quote for a new customer versus a lower margin quote for an existing customer; then, it's really up to your gut instinct to choose which one is more likely to turn into an order.

It is tempting to turn these lists into Top 6, or Top 10, or Next 20, etc., but I would advise against it. The simple reason is that you are no longer focusing as you should, and can easily end up back in that place where work is falling through the cracks. If you can't come up with these two lists, you need to sharpen your analytical skills. Simply put, you must be able to rank quotations in order of importance.

Following this simple strategy helped me increase my order landing rate for my Top 5. I also stopped promising work to new customers that I could not fulfill. If a quote request came in and I knew I was already behind on my top five, only one of three things would happen:

1. I'd take an existing quote off the list and replace it with the new one if I believed my chances of getting that order were higher than the one already on the list. One goes in, another one comes out.
2. I'd tell my manager that I didn't have time for it and that something had to give, hoping that he would assign the new quotation to one of my colleagues.
3. I'd tell the customer that I did not have the capacity to quote the new project at that time, but to please keep me in mind the next time they

needed this product or service. In most cases, getting a straight answer was appreciated more than promising a quotation that never came.

Use alternative one (1) carefully, as it means you are taking out a quotation you believed in up to this point. As said above, the temptation to make the list top 6 is enormous. I'd like to point out that just because a quotation does not make the top 5, it doesn't mean that it's not important or that you aren't going to work on it, it just means that you aren't going to work on it first. Do not make the common mistake of loading yourself to the point where you cannot serve anyone well. Read more about this in the next section.

Exercise reason three (3) with caution. Just because you are busy does not mean everyone else is too busy. The company will most likely want to submit a quote. If it's not you, it can be someone else. Let your manager be the judge and have them make the decision.

## The Smelly Fish Quotation

The smelly fish quotation is the one that has started to smell bad because it's been sitting in your to do pile or in your email folder for so long. You should have done it a long time ago, but for one reason or another you just never got around to it. It's not like there were no opportunities to do it, it's just that there were more important quotes to work on.

If the quotation is only a little late, you can always get in touch with the customer and let them know that you are running behind and either ask for more time or tell them you can't quote this right now. If they are receptive to giving you more time, it can mean that they really are interested in receiving your quotation – a positive sign. If they give you an extension, do not ask for another one. If you do, the customer will feel like you are not prioritizing their business, and the fact is you are not.

Every now and then you will find yourself in a situation where you are so late that you do not even want to call the customer anymore. You suspect that they have already ordered from someone, and by calling them you will just get an earful of your poor performance. So, you don't call them. If you have let the situation get this far, it is very difficult to dig yourself out without causing hard feelings. You are mad at yourself, and the customer is most likely mad at you too; especially, if they waited for you to participate. If they are not mad at you, they may have given up on you. You may have lost more than a quote; you may have lost a customer.

At this point, you have to make a decision if you will proceed with the bid or not. What many salespeople end up doing is throwing together a sloppy quotation and sending it to the customer; mainly to be able to tell their manager that they did it. This is not a good idea. The customer, who already does not think so highly of you, will recognize the quality of your work and will think even less of you after seeing it. Trust me, when the customer receives several quotes, they can see who spent time on it and who didn't. Another alternative is to make a time consuming quotation for them; again, mainly to prove to yourself that you did get it done. You do this even though you don't really expect the customer to get back with you. Well, if this makes you feel better; then, what can I say? I am going to tell you, though, that this does not mitigate the situation at all. The only result is that you waste your valuable time.

Unfortunately, the only way of resolving an issue like this and keeping a potential relationship with this customer is to not let it happen in the first place. But, before you kick yourself too hard, think about this: just the fact that you still have this request in your pile is an indication that you have doubts about this quotation. If it was an existing customer or fit your product perfectly, you would have quoted it a long time ago. Do yourself a favor and at least try to keep the customer relationship by letting them know within a reasonable amount of time that you are passing this time, but want to keep getting requests. Next time, the quote request you receive may be one that really suits your company well.

# 10.

# PRIORITIZING TO MAXIMIZE TIME

Time management is the toughest challenge for the salesperson. There is a lot of work to be done within a limited amount of time, and you have to make sure you are spending that time where it will yield the best results. In Chapter 9, I introduced my Top 5-Next 5 method of ranking quotes to help you spend your work efforts wisely. In this chapter, I will point out common time robbers that make the salesperson less productive. If you recognize a trait in yourself, you can work on rectifying it.

## Common Time Robbers

### I've spent so much time on this that I can't possibly stop now

It happens often; a salesperson has invested so much time in a quotation that they feel there is no choice but to follow it through to the bitter end. They fool themselves into believing there's still a chance of landing it. After all, they put so much work into it …

In business, this is called throwing good money after bad or a sunk cost. Someone has lost their objectivity, and refuses to see the fact that a quote is stale. Just because a salesperson has spent countless hours on a project does not guarantee results. Do not make the mistake of looking back two months from now at the same quotation and realizing you have spent even more time and money on it. Instead, ask for an objective view. Sit down with your manager or coworker and discuss what's going on. If all the evidence points to a situation where you are continuing to work on a case just because you've already expended so much energy on it, it may be time to stop and move on to the next case.

If you look at the reasons you get orders, you will find out that spending an exorbitant amount of time on one quotation is not on the list. Increasing time spent is not necessarily going to increase your chances of landing the order. If the average quote takes one week to make, spending eight weeks on a quote does not increase your chances of getting that order by eight times. Instead, it might be worth doing eight quotes within that same time.

There are three major symptoms of a stale quote:

- The customer has given countless deadlines when a decision will be made. It's always next month, next quarter, next year. It never seems to stop.

- The customer's organization around the quote has not changed for a while. It may seem the contact person is working by themselves on this project. Every now and then we hit a customer who is asking us to quote something just to stay busy themselves. You will know what I mean when you realize you have been working on one of these quotation requests. Unfortunately, there is no way of knowing this when the request arrives. It's only after some digging that you can see if it's the customer's organization or an individual behind the request.

- The customer does not have firm advice about how to revise your quote, or it dramatically changes all the time. They may ask for some changes today, and then ask for different changes a month from now. They may have good intentions, but the project never reaches a critical point where the order is placed.

> I once inherited a salesperson that did not recognize the symptoms of a stale quote. When we first spoke, he was optimistic about Revision 164 of a quote he had been

working on for a *decade*. Yes, over *ten* years. He was an experienced salesperson with a good track record, proving that this can happen to anybody.

This salesman had one main customer. He knew all the right contacts, and had been selling to them for years. The quotation was a *whale*; the huge quote that every salesperson wants to land at least once in their career. So, over the course of ten plus years he revised and rewrote that quotation 164 times, and year after year he told his manager that *soon* the customer will decide. And since he knew everyone at the customer, he was going to get the order *for sure*.

What he failed to grasp was that during that ten year period the customer's organization had changed, and there was an influx of new hires. Over time his pool of decision-making contacts was diluted, yet still he held tight to that shrinking group of people (with diminishing power) that he had worked with for 20 years to help him in the final order decision. All his time was consumed waiting for a phone call from this one customer for the smallest change. He was hardly working with any other customer.

By the time I came along and pulled the plug on the quotation, which I told him I would have done seven to eight years before, he had spent over $1million of company money in salary and travel costs. (I know what you are thinking ... )

I have to commend his skills for selling a dream. The previous manager had already planned how to use all the money that would be made on the sale to expand the business. So, in reality the entire episode was not totally the salesman's fault. His manager should have demanded results, and better penetration into the customer's organization. The manager was so blinded by the size of this quotation that he allowed this to happen.

Needless to say, someone else got the order about a year after I came on board. That someone was a company at least ten times bigger than we were. Some of you are thinking we should have kept trying. But, here's a major problem with the *whale* of a quote: they typically amount to at least one half, maybe several times, the company's yearly turnover. The customer is dealing in reality, and they are not going to place their confidence in a company that does not have the capacity to fulfill their order. It is plain and simple risk management on the customer's side, and is often not recognized by the supplier's sales personnel that are eager to land the whale. The mailbox example from Chapter 1 is a prime illustration of this topic.

## Tinkering with quotations you enjoy

Salespeople tinker with quotations they enjoy, and they are not always the ones that will produce the best results. It's easy to keep talking and quoting small items to an existing, good customer even if the profits are meager. It is not as much work, and the results are, more or less, guaranteed. Since salespeople are human, it is up to their manager to keep the department working toward new customers without forgetting the existing ones. Sales skills need to be practiced. If a salesperson is left to tinker long enough, they will lose the skills and courage to acquire new customers. I've seen salespeople become afraid of the phone after not cold calling for awhile.

## Working on everything that moves

It's tempting to work on every potential request that comes your way. This is a common issue, but in today's world full of competition there aren't many companies that can pull it off. Don't fall into the trap where you are promising everyone something, but can't do a good job on anyone's quote because you don't have the time to concentrate on any of them. It is better to limit your cases and spend enough time on each one so that it is done properly.

It's easy to pump out quotes that include products and services you know well. It can take days or weeks to produce a quote using products and services at the edge of your expertise, and still you will most likely lose the order because you don't have the in depth knowledge about the customer or application.

Again, we come back to the subject of prioritization. It is absolutely mandatory for you to look at your backlog and decide which cases are the best to work on. Set those on top of the pile, and maybe try to pass the bottom ones to your colleagues. (Just keep in mind that when your colleague makes a sale on one of the requests you passed on, you can't be jealous.)

## Internal meetings

Everyone knows the internal meeting is a major time robber. It takes a lot of time, people who are not pertinent to the decision making process are there, and with so many people present the subject easily veers from the main topics. Salespeople tend to be extroverts and like to talk, which leads to lengthy meetings when there are no clear limits. To alleviate this problem, have a set agenda and follow it as closely as possible. Invite only the people relevant to the issues being discussed, and send minutes of meetings to other personnel afterwards.

# Tracking Your Work

Most managers want to have at least a general idea of what their subordinates are working on. Sometimes they will measure productivity by the number of calls made, the number of quotes pushed out, or by total sales or margins. Rarely will anyone track the minute details of the day. So, how do you keep track of who did what, what was said, and when?

For this purpose, I developed a diary that works for me. It's like a closet organizer for my sales activity with space for everything and to record the main events of that day. These events include new quotes and revisions I've promised and when they're due (Told Jack his quote will be there on Wednesday). I write down the quotes where most of my day went, any major changes in a customer's organization, meetings, and phone numbers I received to name a few. I fill it out every day at the end of the day. My diary is a catch all for all information, so I know exactly where to find it when I need it. I always carry it with me.

There are three main reasons for doing this:

1. I want to know where the time goes. You can't tell what you worked on last month, or even last week if you don't remember. I also wanted to see how long the quotes would take from the time they appeared on the Top 5 list to when the customer made a decision.

2. I want a record of questions I answer on the phone, and items and schedules agreed to in case there is a difference of opinion later on. These diaries have saved my rear-end more times than I can count. Sometimes customers remember events or dates differently, but when I can pull out my book and show them in writing that we agreed to this or that on such and such date, it usually ends the misunderstanding quickly and on a good note.

3. The legal aspects of keeping documentation. I am a firm believer in confirming everything – a phone conversation or meeting – in writing. If things ever get really bad, these records can be used in the court of law as evidence. Of course, no one wants to think they will ever end up in a situation to use these documents, but they are available if it ever happens.

# PART V:
# THE CUSTOMER

# 11.

# LISTEN TO THE CUSTOMER

When we were young our elders often told us that there is a reason why we have two ears and only one mouth. This same advice works well when dealing with customers. Customers are dying to tell you what is going on. You just have to let them. Listen and let the customer do the talking as much as possible. There's a general misconception that the best salespeople are extroverted fast-talkers. It isn't true. If you love hearing yourself talk, be ready for a mediocre sales career. If you can be humble, ask the right questions, and get answers without upsetting anyone in the process, you can become great.

In this chapter, we will discuss the customer's motives behind the buying process, customer evaluation and product selection as a team effort, and who really makes the decision to order.

## Why Do Customers Buy From You?

Companies want to know why customers buy their products because the data is very valuable. They send mails and emails: "Dear customer, would you please tell us why you decided to buy from us?" Websites ask for feedback even though response rates may be low, and customers can get irritated with seemingly endless questionnaires and surveys with no apparent benefit to them.

Feedback is great with one exception: it tends to come only from certain minded people when what a company needs is a wide variety of opinions. Personally, I do not trust these survey results any more than I trust Yelp reviews. Basing decisions on skewed results built on bad data does not work. My data is good because I collect it directly, and I don't use filters during the data collection process. Let's see how data can be used in the right way:

> Ted owns a gym in a town with five or six other gyms. His prices are more expensive ($70/month) than any other gym in town, and the gym has made a loss for the past two years. He has a loyal group of members, but it is just too small to cover expenses and leave some profit. Ted needs reliable information about why his customers are his customers and how to attract more of their kind, so he decides to interview existing members.
>
> In exchange for a 15 minute interview, participants receive $15 off next month's membership fee. During the interview, Ted fills out a form based on market specific information, and asks participants for their opinions and recommendations. When the interview process is over, Ted knows his members and his members know him. They also feel included; Ted cares about what they want. Because his members feel they know Ted better as a person, they are less likely to leave the gym.
>
> The process costs Ted money, but the goodwill and information he generates is worth it. Because Ted took the trouble of conducting all the interviews himself, he knows the data is good. Now, he can start looking at the characteristics of his customers and find what is important to them. This information can be used in new customer acquisition, and developing his gym for his core user.

Ted could have spent $2,000 on a gym report, but the data would not be as reliable as what he collected himself.

I would claim that the biggest reason customers buy from someone is because they have purchased from that supplier before. They have a positive feeling about the company, and have no real reason to look for anyone else. Their needs are being met and it is easy. In order for them to look at other alternatives, there must be a trigger that sets the search in motion.

Another reason people buy is because they have heard that a product is good. A friend, family member, coworkers, or even complete strangers on a bulletin board can affect choices. People ask for opinions about products and services on online discussion boards all the time. It's easier to take someone else's word for a product or service, rather than spend a lot of time researching and comparing when they're in a hurry. If someone else has already purchased the product and they are happy with it, why wouldn't I be happy too?

Sometimes it is plain old price that matters. People buy based on what they can afford or what they are willing to pay. I make the distinction because it's never wise to assume that just because someone is frugal – or outright cheap – that they are poor. Even penny-pinchers are willing to spend money on something they like.

Often people kick themselves after buying a cheap product (I do not mean inexpensive, but cheap – like I did with my drill.) with the expectations that it will last for a long time. Think flat box furniture. It is inexpensive to buy, easy to assemble, but not that easy to move from one location to another. At the time of a move they become cheap. A little moving and shaking and it seems like every nail is coming apart. However, at the time of purchase, price is a compelling argument. If I paid $300 for a bookshelf versus $2,000 for a bookshelf, the difference is

$1,700 of hard earned cash in my hand. It's money that I can use somewhere else, or money that I don't have to borrow. If I buy the $300 bookshelf now and have to move, I'll just buy another one. And still, I'll spend less than one half of the more expensive bookshelf. Maybe next time I'll have more money and can consider getting the nice one then. And so it goes. This very same thinking applies to companies too.

> I was working with a mill in Canada. The company was known for their tight budgeting. A piece of equipment they were looking to fix was total junk and costing them a lot of money. I priced out a new piece of equipment, and the price came to $54,000. The purchasing agent was very apologetic as he explained to me that they could not purchase new equipment because the budget was not for a new piece of equipment. It was to fix the old equipment. He said he had up to $79,000 to refurbish the existing equipment. He guided me to use some parts of the existing equipment, change my bid to read *refurbish the equipment* (instead of quoting new equipment), and keep the price the same.

Sometimes there are funny things at play. If the customer didn't tell me the budgeting situation, I wouldn't have been able to provide a bid that suited their needs.

Availability can be a determining factor in a purchase. As many businesses have decreased their inventories, more and more often there are customers ready and willing to buy on the spot because they need or want a product immediately, but can't because the seller doesn't have it on hand. These customers don't want to wait for the item to be shipped in 2-5 days, 1-2 weeks, or 3-4 months. They want it no later than tomorrow. There are companies that have created a competitive edge by keeping good inventories on hand for immediate delivery. Usually, the customer pays more to have their product now. They know it, and they accept it.

A customer may buy a product for prestige. This is why you don't see many millionaires driving around in Kia's or Hyundai's. (Sorry Kia and Huyndai!) This does not mean that Kia or Hyundai are bad cars; they simply do not have the same prestige value as Porsche or Ferrari.

The bottom line is it doesn't matter why someone buys from you as long as they do. But, knowing why they do helps you capture more customers and increase your profits as well as make sure you hold on to those good customers.

## Why Customers Don't Buy From You

It's easy talking to customers who buy from you. Analyzing why a customer did not buy from you can feel like an unpleasant, negative task, but it has to be done. Luckily, if you are able, this is a good task to outsource to a neutral party because the customer is more likely to be candid with them anyway.

There are many reasons why a customer does not buy from a supplier, but here are some of the more common ones:

- They don't know a company is offering a product or service
- They have had a bad experience with a company
- They are happy with their current supplier
- They have integrated the current supplier into their organization, and changing would be costly and time consuming
- The supplier's location is too far away
- They have doubts about the potential supplier

It's possible that customers don't even know that you provide a service they need, and they buy from someone else. This is common, and is why companies should always get the word out there. Marketing, marketing, marketing – it works.

Customers may have tried a company in the past and had an unpleasant experience. It's a tough job to win them back when they have a sour taste in their mouth. One possible fix is changing the person responsible for that account. Try something new. What do you have to lose at this point? Another alternative is to straight out ask for another opportunity. It's surprising how often this works. It doesn't mean that a supplier has to beg on their knees, it just means that they acknowledge they screwed up before, and they understand that the customer is a bit hesitant, but they'd like a second chance to show how they can do a good job. (Screw up that second chance and it will take a miracle for you to get a third chance.)

As said earlier, a customer does not change suppliers without a reason; a trigger. Sometimes the trigger is obvious. Other times the trigger is an unconscious one; they can't pinpoint why they are unhappy with their current supplier, they just are. It could be a collection of small things. If a customer is upset or disappointed with their current supplier, it's an opportunity for another supplier to swoop in and win them over.

If the customer is happy with their existing supplier and sees no reason to go through the hassle of changing over to a new one, in my experience, there must be a significant price difference for them to change suppliers strictly based on price. If you are offering a comparable product with a comparable price, you will need some other feature or added value to act as a trigger for change.

## Customer Motives for Buying

If you can find the motives for why or how a customer purchases, you have found the key to unlocking the sale. However, the motives are not always clear to the salesperson that sees and hears only part of the buying related information.

## Buying Security from Big Companies

If a customer is not buying a low price, most times they are buying a peace of mind. If the customer's buying team proposes to senior management that the company purchase a project from the perceived largest supplier company in the field, they expect to get security. The customer probably knows that they can get the items in question at a less expensive price from somewhere else, but the underlying feeling is that unless there is a great technological advantage in the other products, why take the risk? The decision is made easier when company, and not their own, funds are at stake.

Below are reasons why a customer wants to buy from the biggest company:

- Larger companies have been around longer. They are well established, and they have staying power. Small companies can go bankrupt overnight; their key personnel can move to another company leaving the small company in a lurch, etc.

- The perception that if something goes wrong with a product or delivery, a big company is better equipped to stand behind their promises than a small company.

These are some of the most important psychological facts affecting a competitive sales situation, and they have a direct effect on how a customer regards potential suppliers throughout the sales cycle.

## Buying from One of the Other Companies

Below are the reasons why a customer chooses a smaller company:

- Price
- Better technology

- Close relationship between the customer and the supplier. It can include physical, personnel, personal, and even ownership.

## Price

Price is a sensitive subject. Even the leading or perceived biggest company must be somewhat price competitive in order to get the sale. Over the years, I have seen that the typical price spread that the customer will accept between the leading company and a solid #2 bidder maxes out somewhere between 8%-12%, assuming they believe that the #2 bidder can perform equally as well as #1.

If an alternative supplier can show acceptable technology, good references, meet all other requirements, and the price spread exceeds 20%, they are almost guaranteed to get an order. The customer's purchasing team reports to layers of management. Reporting is based only on numbers with some side notes, so unless the team can come up with a solid reason why to buy from the most expensive option, they are almost obligated to buy from the cheaper price alternative. If the team chooses to pay excessively more than what is available from others, their motives can be questioned.

## Technology

Usually during the quotation phase of a larger project, the customer's technical team is in charge of the specification work. Their goal is to make sure that every bidder moving forward in the process has an at least minimum acceptable technical solution to their problem. They weed out companies that they feel may not be reliable.

One way a smaller company can stay competitive is by constant advancements in technology. Sometimes being an early adaptor works well; sometimes it leads to bankruptcy. If an early adapter company can present a technological solution where the required capacity or output is reached with a smaller investment on the customer's part, perhaps through a patented method or through significantly lower operating costs, they have a good chance of receiving an order. Again, it falls back on price. The total price or price per unit is lower.

It is also entirely possible that the price is more. If a new technology achieves a new level of capacity or output allowing the customer to expand into new markets, the product can be desirable in spite of a higher price.

## Closeness

I deliberately chose the word *closeness* for this section, instead of location, because closeness can mean different things:

- A supplier is physically located close to the customer, sometimes under the same roof.
- Businesses are linked together by ownership ties.
- The top managers of two companies are close friends, went to the same school, or have the same financier, etc.

Physical closeness is obvious for any salesperson to see. The other relationships are not obvious, and can be hard to find.

> I visited a mill in Indiana that split part of its business from the rest of operations, and formed a separate business entity. The new entity was still located within the customer's buildings, and it employed the same personnel as before the split. The purchasing department for the mill was still obligated to get three vendor quotes for the products and services the new entity provided, but it was clear to anyone who understood the situation which company would win the order.

Experience may be your only teacher in finding this information, but it always pays to ask questions. The answers are all clues.

- Do you use more than one vendor for this product?
- Who have you done business with before?
- How long have you done business with them?
- Why are you doing business with them?
- Who else, in the same field, have you done business with?

## Team Purchasing

Purchasing a large project is rarely decided by one person. The CEO may sign the deal in front of the cameras, but the evaluation and decision making process is almost always a team effort.

# 12.

# PENETRATING THE CUSTOMER ORGANIZATION

## Width x Depth = Sales

In order to have a chance of selling to the team you need two dimensions to your selling effort: *width and depth*. Both the decision and evaluation are most likely made by a group of people from different disciplines – construction, electrical, IT. The width of your selling effort will include getting to know the representatives from each of these disciplines that are working directly on the purchasing team. The depth of your selling effort will mean getting to know the many layers of organization within each separate discipline. This includes people who may be decision makers, but are not involved in day to day discussions. It may also include people who, seemingly at the time of the purchase, have no decision making powers at all. For example, the project engineer, the project manager, the senior project manager, and the VP of finance.

## The Whisperer

It is very difficult to know which discipline has more vendor or product selection power than others. It could be the finance people, operations, maintenance, or even the CEO. All disciplines have powerful advisers behind the scenes: *the whisperers*. These folks lean on the decision makers behind the scenes, and try to affect the outcome of a purchase without anyone outside the company knowing they are part of the decision making process.

In the Volvo example in Chapter 7, the maintenance supervisor is the whisperer. He is trying to convince the project team to buy his preferred product, Volvo trucks, but he is not an obvious decision maker. It is the fear of potential recurring future costs (additional labor, training, and spare parts) versus a one-time truck purchase cost that gives the maintenance supervisor the power to be a whisperer.

It is very important that one of the first things you do when pursuing a sale is identify all the whisperers. Next, find out their position on each supplier, and do your best to influence them to not be against your product or company. Don't make the mistake of concentrating only on the managers within your direct circle. You never know whose help you may need later on in the bidding process, and you don't want to lose an order because you didn't know about a whisperer.

## Why Three Neutrals Are Better Than Two For's and One Against

You are probably wondering why I'm telling you that at this point in the bidding process that it's important to make sure no one feels strongly against your product or company. How are you ever going to win a bid if everyone isn't 100% for your product and company?

My father told me something when I was first starting out in sales: you don't need everyone cheering for you, you just can't have anyone feeling strongly against you. That was over two decades ago, and I still haven't met anyone who has voiced this idea more simply or correctly.

This issue is highly psychological, as described earlier. Once people form an opinion of a product, company, or salesperson they tend to stick to it no matter what. This can appear as passive-aggressive behavior. Neutral's, on the other hand, are a clean slate to work with and can be swayed much easier.

# PENETRATING THE CUSTOMER ORGANIZATION 133

I was working with a company in Detroit. The project engineer had heard from our competitor that my equipment was unreliable. It didn't matter what I told him, his opinion was firm. In order to circumvent him, I went to the manager and asked him to visit our reference. I wanted them to see our product for themselves. The manager delegated the visit to the above mentioned project engineer. A visit was set for two weeks later. A few days before the visit, the project engineer informed us that due to his schedule, the visit had to be postponed for an additional two weeks. This happened over and over. The project engineer did finally visit the reference, but in his own words, "It wasn't that impressive," even though it was the most technologically advanced equipment on the market.

If someone is a firm *against*, they are almost impossible to turn to a *positive*. If we had an unlimited amount of time and money, maybe we could have turned this engineer to a *neutral*.

Unfortunately, I haven't always taken this advice. When I was starting out, there were times when I either forgot to keep my eye on the process, or was too cocky thinking I had already landed a sale before the order. I got upset with customer's behavior and just had to show my displeasure. Apparently, I was the type of young man that needed to learn on my own, and now I can say there's nothing like the embarrassment of a few disastrous quotes and sales cases to pound a truth into your head. I share my experience here in the hopes that you will benefit from my mishaps and avoid your own.

I've also fallen into the same trap as other salespeople, and found it easier to work only with the people I clicked with and trusted within a customer's organization. If you meet with a purchasing team and find out that Jim and Debbie are on your side, but that Jack and Bill are leaning toward your competitor, it's natural that you will be inclined to work with Jim and Debbie. You trust and hope that they can convince Jack and Bill to choose you instead. Sometimes this works, but sometimes it does not. If you want to increase your chances for a sale, start working with Jack and Bill, as well. Include them in the process and ask their opinions. Find out their reservations and serve them so well that they move from the opposing camp to undecided or indifferent. There's a lot less space to negotiate between an "indifferent" and a "yes" than there is between a "no" and a "yes." Meanwhile don't forget Jim and Debbie, but remember they should not be the only ones tended.

In the beginning, Jack and Bill may think that your interest is somewhat fake; you are just trying to win them over. However, if you keep working with them, there is a good chance they will end up indifferent or even in your camp. This is an area where you can see a big difference between sales pros and sales novices.

Again, not everyone on the team must be your avid supporter, but you can't afford to have anyone strongly opposed to ordering from you either. Indifferent is Ok.

## Keeping the Customer's Trust

Your main task as the quotation leader is to make sure there are zero doubts on the customer's side about anything. Customer doubts are like tree roots growing into a house's foundation. As time goes by, the roots get bigger and bigger creating enough damage, so that eventually they take out the entire foundation. Just about any little thing can create a hairline crack in this sensitive area. Losing your cool at a meeting, not explaining your point clearly, not providing information in a timely manner, providing incomplete information, or even using the wrong expert from your company in a presentation can create a small doubt about your organization's ability to serve this customer better than the competitors. Scrutinize each piece of information before you give it to the customer to make sure there is nothing that can be misunderstood because you may not get a second chance to explain it. This is particularly true when dealing with people who are leaning toward your competitors, or people you haven't dealt with much. They tend to read information with a different mindset than the people who are in your camp.

If this does happen and you find yourself bumped out of the lead bidding position, it's time to take a timeout and figure out what needs to be done to get back into the game. Call your trusted supporter at the customer's (hopefully, you have one), invite them to lunch, and ask for some advice. You just might get it. Analyze the case and see if there is something you need to change. Time is of the essence, and the worst thing you can do is nothing. The more time that goes by, the stronger the opponent's position becomes. Act quickly.

## Decision Makers

A lot of sales books advise the reader how to sell to the C-Suite. In most cases, I have my suspicions about how many large company CEOs these guys are hanging with. I realize that after reading these books your excitement meter is hitting 100%, but do you really expect to pick up the phone and call Coca Cola's headquarters and open the conversation like this? "This is John Smith. I am sales director at Eastern LOAF Trucking. We are bidding on some of your transportation routes in Kentucky. May I speak with your CEO?" That is a short phone call, wouldn't you agree? Yes, CEO's are involved in some deals, but unless you are selling a huge ticket item to Coca Cola do not expect to speak with or meet the CEO. And if you insist upon it, you may look like an idiot. This is just the way it is.

It's been my experience that as the importance of the purchase increases and the dollar amounts rise, the bigger the titles that get involved with a project. I worked on a sale of approximately $40million. At that time my sales team and I did meet the CEO, and did not get the sale. In another instance I had a quote of approximately $22million, never met the CEO, and did get the order. Keep in mind that at some companies it may very well be the buyer, office manager, or project engineer who is your main contact, and they can be responsible for relatively large budgets.

A good way to find out if your contact has decision making authority is to ask them if they need anyone else's approval to place the order. They know why you ask, and if you don't throw them under the bus they don't mind. We all have managers, or as one acquaintance put it, "We all, regardless of our titles, are someone's secretary."

## Closing Notes on Decision Makers

When weaving your web of contacts throughout a customer's organization, do not forget to consider any of the separate disciplines. Purchasing teams can consist of multiple departments, and they all have some say in the final decision. You need to cover everyone, no exceptions.

Do not make the mistake of choosing to only speak with the decision maker or your main contact; consequently, giving an impression, intentionally or unintentionally, that you are ignoring everyone else in a meeting. This happens a lot with car salespeople who are starting out. They may prefer to speak with the husband, even if the wife could easily be the whisperer or decision maker. Never assume that someone is not important, no matter what their title. Often folks with lesser titles attend meetings too. Even if they have no visible organizational power, decision makers may listen to their opinion. If someone is in a meeting, they are there because they matter, or because the company is investing in their training because they think that they will matter in the future. Either way, you may need these people on your side. Also, you never know who may be able to help you later on. Respect everyone. You will create a good impression of yourself, your company, and your product.

Before a project goes to final decision you will need to know the decision makers and the whisperers within each department, and what affects their decisions. What is important to them?

## It's OK to Take No for an Answer

You know what? It is OK to take no for an answer. It's ridiculous to think that every contact you make will turn to a customer. Following is an example.

> Let's say Nitesh gets hired as a realtor. He is eagerly cold calling a list of residents in his town to promote his services. When Nitesh calls Carl, who is also a realtor, what are the chances of Nitesh making a sale or starting a customer-realtor relationship? None. And it doesn't matter if Nitesh has decided that under no circumstances will he take "no" for an answer.

My point here is that you can't sell to everyone. In the example above, Nitesh might find a customer here and there, but absolutely none of those customers will include other realtors. Also, people who just bought a home are not worth spending a lot of time on. In other words, they do not have an actual or perceived need for what Nitesh is selling. Even though they are a potential customer, he will not turn them into customers.

Similarly, for each product or service a salesperson tries to sell there are certain groups of prospects who appear as potential customers, but are not.

## Classifying Customers

I love hearing the salesperson that brags how they can sell anything to anyone. Good for them. (Insert sarcasm here.) As for the rest of us salespeople who simply aren't *that* good, here is what I do. I divide potential customers into five different categories based on how I perceive the possibility of selling to them:

1. Already a customer, or a strong contender to become a customer
2. Potentially a customer, or already an infrequent customer
3. Could become a customer
4. More likely will not become a customer
5. Very low chance of becoming a customer

Within these categories, available time should be spent something like this.

| | | |
|---|---|---|
| 1. | Already a customer or a strong contender to become a customer | ~ 60% of time |
| 2. | Potentially a customer or infrequent customer | ~ 30% of time |
| 3. | Could become a customer | < 10% of time |
| 4. | More likely will not become a customer | < 5% of time |
| 5. | Very low chance of becoming a customer | < 1% of time |

If you discover some qualifying facts indicating that someone is not going to be your customer (categories 4 and 5), in my opinion, it is much better time management to just take no from them. For the busy salesperson the scarcest resource is time. Time has to be utilized in a way that produces the best possible results. Even category 3 is often not worth investing excessive time and effort. Sometimes there is a jewel buried in the mud of category 3, but it takes a lot of time finding one, and the results are questionable. Instead, spend the majority of your time on categories 1 and 2.

Most salespeople automatically manage their time like this. It is mentioned here so you can recognize when you find yourself spending a lot of time on the #3, #4, and #5 categories. Every now and then, check where your time goes and make the necessary adjustments. Of course, this theory does not hold exactly the same if your job is new customer acquisition because you don't have existing customers to work with, but still it is pretty close.

# 13.

# WHAT'S REALLY GOING ON?

## The Brush-Off

For one reason or another, a customer is giving you the brush-off. It may be passive – not answering or turning away when you try to catch up with them or talk. It can be a polite hint, or a more direct one. It may even seem a bit harsh in the way they make it clear they don't want to talk to you. And, it may be just as uncomfortable for them as it is for you.

A customer initiates the brush-off because they don't want to engage themselves, or they want to end the sales discussion they are already engaged in. Period. It can be for any number of reasons that have nothing to do with the salesperson or the product being sold. Maybe the customer has a dentist appointment and they don't want to share that information, it's time to pick up the kids, the post office is about to close. It may have nothing to do with the salesperson, but to the salesperson it appears that it has everything to do with them, and the brush-off can easily be misunderstood.

The brush-off can also be directly related to the sales process. The customer changed their mind about buying, they don't like the product, they can't afford it, or they already bought from someone else. Maybe they just don't like the salesperson.

There can be numerous reasons why a customer brushes you off, but the *way* a customer brushes you off is usually dependent on personality.

Some people simply can't say no, and it makes them easy prey for ruthless salespeople. They may want a salesperson to go away, but they don't have it in them to tell them to. This person may feel so awkward and want so desperately to avoid a conflict, they might buy a product they don't want or need. We've all heard at least one story of someone being taken advantage of by an unscrupulous salesperson. The elderly often fall into this category. For the record, I will never stoop so low to take advantage of someone who clearly can't defend themselves, and will never condone that lack of integrity in anyone else. I'm sure you won't either.

Some people were brought up to be very soft-spoken, and to not get upset with anyone. They try to tell the salesperson, using soft and polite words, that they are not interested by attempting to excuse themselves from the situation, but some salespeople just do not want to get the message. They misunderstand these signals and follow the customer around or keep calling them still trying to make the sale, and the customer is too polite to end it. These people feel intimidated by pushy salespeople, and often cannot articulate clearly and firmly why they are not interested.

In-between types of people swing back and forth between yes and no, and end up with maybe. Their brush off is weak because they actually may want to buy; they just don't know how to go about it. It's possible they want something that they can't have because it's out of stock or out of their budget, and they refuse to face the fact. These people can take hours from the salesperson's time; then, change their mind just like that.

Unyielding people tell the salesperson that they are not interested, and that's that. They usually can give a good reason, as well. Since they are articulate about their reasoning, the salesperson may try to take one last stab at it, but are quickly shut down by the customer. These customers are somewhat easy for the salesperson because they are easy to read. No is no, and it will not be unclear.

The last personality type hates all salespeople. They seem to think that every salesperson lies just to get them to spend more money. They can be rude, and always seem to have a bad attitude. What these people fail to comprehend is that every now and then even they need a knowledgeable salesperson to assist them. Their brush off can be harsh, but perhaps harsher than they intended, which makes them tough to read.

Regardless of the type of brush-off, always keep your composure. It is always better to part on good terms, no matter how disappointed you are at the time. You can still ask if it is ok to contact the customer at a future time to further discuss the product. They may not want you to, but then again they just may. At this point, you lose nothing by asking. It's definitely not the time to push the customer because you feel you deserve some sort of compensation after spending so much time with them. Just thank them for their time, repeat your name, and tell them that when the time comes you hope you can be of service to them.

## Ability to Squeeze a Decision

At some point in the sales process, you will need to push the customer to make up their mind up. This is easier said than done, and it varies greatly from one product and industry to another.

In small sales it can be easy. At the coffee shop counter when you see a customer eyeing a jar of cookies, but clearly struggling with himself whether to take one or not, you can say, "Would you like to try one of these delicious cookies with your coffee?" In bigger sales you have less power to affect this timing. Basically, the customer makes a decision when they are good and ready. At the same time, with bigger sales and longer sales processes customers leave more clues along the way that they are or aren't ready to close – they need board approval, site approval, etc.

As you squeeze a decision from the customer keep in mind that it may not be the one you want to hear. You do not have to like it, but you do have to accept it. No matter how disappointed you are, this is a good time to remember that absolutely no one will turn 100% of their quotations into sales. Treating the customer well and presenting yourself well should earn you the chance to make a future sale with the same company or person. Next time, they may buy from you.

The most successful sales professionals are the ones who, time after time, can pump themselves up for the next sales case after losing an order. They know that there are many factors that influence a customer's decision to buy. They also know that even though they lost a sale, the customer may be talking to other people about them. An optimistic, professional attitude can ensure that the talk is positive, and can inadvertently send other customers their way. Never underestimate positive word of mouth as a sales tool.

If you still feel compelled to pout and show your disappointment, remember that when we have a positive experience we tell only a few people. If we have a negative experience, we tell just about anyone who is willing to listen. You really can't afford that.

Here is my rule for squeezing a decision:

When you reach the point where you feel you have used all your sales tools, and there is nothing more to say that can sell your product or service, it's time to politely ask for a decision from the customer. Plan what you will say.

- All your questions and concerns have been answered, and there seems no reason to delay a decision …
- I know this is a big decision, but it won't get any easier with time …
- Should we shake hands and do the paperwork?

- If you have something preventing you from placing the order, would you please share it with me, so I can address it right away?

There is nothing wrong in asking for the customer to make up their mind. Sometimes the customer needs that final push. If you do not push them and let them leave the situation, they may not come back, and your competitor may be successful in closing the sale.

## The Cold Shoulder Treatment

There are times when it feels like a customer is giving you the cold shoulder. For some reason, unknown to you, they are no longer answering your emails or returning your calls. No one sees this as good news. Still, it is possible that the customer is busy and simply does not have time to get back with you, or they don't have any news for you and deem it a waste of time to call. This is not so bad. The remaining alternatives are not so good.

If this happens to you, keep sending emails to the customer at a reasonable interval – say once per week. These emails should be polite, and ask the customer to get in touch with you to let you know the status of the quotation. Also, call and leave messages about once per week. Sooner or later, they should pick up the phone. If several weeks go by and they have not; then, you *know* that they have no intentions of picking up the phone. The good news is that many times the situation is interpreted as worse than it really is, and can be solved on a phone call.

If a customer does not pick up the phone or answer your emails for a length of time, you can assume that the deal is lost. Sometimes the customer is not inclined to tell you the real story about what happened, so they give you an excuse. It's usually quite simple and easy. *It was your price. You were much more expensive than the prevailing bid.* If it's not the price; then, it's the delivery. *We needed it next week and you could not do it.* Sometimes it's the product itself. No other direct reasons are usually given, but I would dare to claim that it is not always the price or availability. Sometimes the customer just likes the other company or their personnel more. Maybe they got a bad vibe from a salesperson or company. They didn't appreciate a slow response time, or the product quoted was wrong for them. It could have been anything, and it may not even be anything negative about you, but something positive about the other supplier. It is very difficult to dig and find the *real* reasons why you lose an order, and as said before, many times the customer can't pinpoint an absolute reason either.

The bottom line is that until a customer tells you that it is over as far as you are concerned it's not over. Never give up on a hunch or feeling. It is not unreasonable at all to expect that a customer will let you know if they are interested or not in ordering from you.

As a closing note, always remember that even if you received the cold shoulder treatment from a customer on a previous bid, you can't hold it against them in future dealings. The past is past, and if you want any chance of building or keeping a relationship with the customer, you do not bring this subject up at all. Treat every quote request as a possibility to do business, and that's that. Holding grudges will get you absolutely nowhere!

## The Rule of Non-Negotiation

Over my career, I have developed the Rule of Non-Negotiation. Simply put: if the customer is buying and they are no longer seriously negotiating with you, they are negotiating with your competitor. This can happen at any phase in the sales process. The fact is the customer can't buy from all bidders, so early on in the process they start eliminating candidates and continue until there is only one left.

Why were you purged? A wrong answer to the customer and they put you on hold. They thought your company couldn't perform a particular line item on the bid request, or your company was so busy that you couldn't meet the delivery time. Maybe you left an impression of disinterest. Sometimes the elimination is based on a misunderstanding. Another possibility is someone got upset over something you said or presented. There are a hundred and one reasons why this could happen, and unfortunately, many sales professionals go through their entire career without even realizing when it does – or that it happens at all.

The recognizable symptoms of non-negotiation:

- Delayed or non-responsiveness to emails and phone calls
- Lack of time to meet face-to-face
- Any other stalling technique that keeps you at arms' length
- The general feeling of the *cold shoulder*

In the earlier phases of the quotation process, this is poisonous. During the final phases of the quotation process, it is outright lethal because you may not have enough time to recover from it.

You may be able to claw your way back in if this happens in the earlier phases. So, if you sense the symptoms of non-negotiating, do not wait. If there are other people in the customer's organization you can contact, do it. Quickly. Your goal is to set up a phone call, email, or a meeting where you can clarify the misunderstanding, or give the answers the customer is waiting for. This must happen at the speed of light. Every day you delay creates a bigger and bigger distance between the two of you, and at some point the hammer will fall: the polite but firm email or phone call saying that, "We have decided to continue with other companies at this time." In most instances, this ends the game. The customer has discussed these issues among their purchasing or project team, and now everyone, at least officially, is of the same opinion that you are not their vendor. Clawing your way back in is a losing battle.

Be careful not to push too aggressively. You don't want to upset the customer, and spoil the possibility of future sales. Remember, this is only one sale. A long lasting relationship with this customer is more important.

It's crucial that you understand what's going on *before* the hammer falls. Again, if the customer isn't talking to you, they have made a mental decision at this time to proceed with someone else. Usually, this occurs when there are serious differences between the leading quotation and yours, and the customer has decided that you are out. Or, as mentioned above, there is a misunderstanding of your offering. Learn to read the signs before the point of no return.

## Winning an Invitation to the Final Meeting

In larger sales situations; suddenly, before the invitation to a final meeting everything is a rush. The customer is asking for refinements to your bid and very detailed information. What this should tell you is that they are putting together a final specification to be attached to the purchase order. At this point, everything is a go for the customer. Things can't happen fast enough for them to place the order. They could be talking to others too, but the good news is that you definitely know they are talking to you, and there's a real chance you can win the order. You can feel it. The adrenaline is pumping. Your blood pressure goes up and your palms feel sweaty. It's time to rally the troops and put the back office on call. Information needs to turn around as soon as possible because every hour counts. If the customer hasn't invited you to a final onsite meeting yet, it's coming soon. This is a fragile time in the sales cycle. It is the scene leading to the climax.

Meanwhile, some of your competitors are the victims of non-negotiation. No one at the customer has time to talk to them. "They are all in a meeting and won't take my calls. I don't have a good feeling about this," says the competitor's experienced sales manager. "We have to hit them with everything we've got." They are trying very hard to break your dominance because they also are seasoned sales professionals, and they can feel the order slipping away. They're dreading the hammer.

If you find yourself in this camp, it's time to regroup. The salesperson calls his contacts at the customer, the director of sales calls his contacts, and quite often if the deal is a significant one, the sales director asks the CEO to *make the call*. At this point, you will do *anything* to not lose this order, and you make it clear to the customer. It's OK to sound alarmed because you are, but you can't sound desperate or aggravated. No one wants to help a desperate or aggravated person, but genuinely concerned? Maybe. You pull all the stops. After all, your company has spent time and money making this quotation. What are another few phone calls? The success rate for turning a customer at this point is very low, but it has happened. And it will happen again. Statistics are not on your side, but you would love to be that one who beats the numbers.

## The Final Meeting

Congratulations! You have done well to get your company this far.

Now is the time to go over your quotation once again, especially the pricing and responsibilities portions of it. Start looking at the price with a plan of how low you can, or are willing, to go. Any areas requiring work should be clarified. Some responsibilities can have a significant impact on price. Find out the discount value of these items if they are removed during the final meeting. It may get you the order.

Orders of a large magnitude are rarely placed by phone call or email. They are almost always placed in a face-to-face meeting with a handshake. This is a big deal for the supplier, and it usually is a big deal for the customer, as well.

The customer will retain the top two, possibly three, candidates until the bitter end if it is a close race between vendors, the value of the order is large, and the customer's technical team is indifferent or doesn't want to reveal their favorite potential supplier. This is meant to keep bidders aware of the fact that they have not won the order yet.

By inviting more than one party to the final meeting, the customer's intent is very simple: put pressure on all bidders to take up any slack in the price or delivery time. The final meeting can be a very good pay-per-hour scenario for the customer because the price can go down significantly. The remaining bidders all know that during that meeting a decision will be made; one bidder will walk away with an order and the remaining one(s) will go home and lick their wounds.

As explained earlier, when an order is significant, the bidder's entire sales team handling the customer is put on high alert during the final meeting. This happens because if your company cannot meet the price level that the customer has in mind, they may start giving you alternatives as take-offs and add-ons to the bid. If they remove an item, what is the new price? If they add just one item, what is the additional cost? (This may be done just to see how much individual items really cost, so they can be compared to the competitors' similar features.)

The final meeting is often a pure price race, and you better hope that you've done your homework about what to include in your quotation and cost calculation. You should also have a good idea of what products your competitor is offering, and the price level. If you have more items or content in your quotation than your competitor's, you may be selling the project too cheap. On the other hand, if you have been able to create a solution to your customer's problem that requires fewer items than your competitors, you may have a good chance of getting the order with better than average profit. After all, the customer doesn't care how exactly you solve their problem if they are buying a solution, and not just a list of parts. If you know your competitor's products, you should have a good idea of the price level. This is important to know. Always remember, the customer is trying to buy the best solution for the best price. The customer's best case scenario is that you are already the lowest bidder, but through the fear of losing the order you keep lowering your price, effectively competing against yourself. Having an idea of the competition's price can help you prevent this from happening.

I have been told many times at a final meeting, "Your pals from XXX Company are in the next room over recalculating their offer and calling their boss for permission to give a steeper discount. Are you sure you don't need some time to do the same?" This is a buyer's typical technique for pushing you to *make the call.* They know that this is potentially a big deal for your company, and that you have your organizational limitations as far as discounts or pricing overall are concerned. They want you to make the call to your manager, his manager, or the person high enough in your organization to get permission for the biggest and fattest discounts. Sometimes the call is made just to show the buyer that, "See, I am making the call," even if the price level and discounts have been decided in advance.

If at the end of grueling meetings you receive the order, great. Congratulations! Enjoy your victory.

If you lost, you are probably thinking all that work was for nothing. Some people, not the most optimistic ones, figure that second place is just the first and biggest of the losers, but I don't agree with them at all and this is why.

> In 1996, I was in a final meeting in Indonesia for a large project. Eight suppliers were invited. The customer had us all sit in the hallway, side by side, so we all knew who was there. Every day, the customer told us to come back tomorrow morning at 9:00am, since they hadn't had time to discuss the part of the project we were

bidding. The original time schedule was one week. This went on for six weeks. As days went by, the supplier count dropped. After three weeks, there were only three of us left. All the others had given up. After six weeks, the customer finally had time for us. The sale was awarded to someone else. It was a long trip home. A year later, I was the winner of another multi-million dollar order from the same customer. It's reasonable to believe I got it partially because the customer already knew me, and I wasn't starting from ground zero. During the six weeks waiting for those first meetings, we met with several of the customer's decision makers, and had a chance to get to know them personally. And, because we were one of the final bidders on that other project, the customer knew we were already prequalified.

Disappointment is painful. But as I've said before, shake it off like a wet dog. Every time you find yourself in front of the customer is an opportunity to get to know the people within that organization. You have learned something about your competitor, their sales style, and product offering. Next time you will know what you are up against, and the outcome just might be different.

# 14.

# ANALYZING CUSTOMERS

Sales is a constant state of analysis.

- What does the customer want?
- How am I meeting that need?
- Does the customer prefer my offering, or are they indifferent?
- How can I improve my chances of getting this order?

Your job as a salesperson is to take in all this information, analyze it, and plan a course of action based on it. Often we, as customers, meet salespeople who are clearly unhappy with their jobs. They are just going through the motions. When I see people like this, I feel like giving them a shake, "Wake up, stop moping, and take control of your sales job." (For the record, I don't actually go around doing that.)

The first layer of scrutiny happens at the market level. Not every customer is for you, your product, or for your company. You need to know who your target market customers are – the ones most likely to order from you – and decide if it is worth your time, at this time, to pursue this customer. Never forget that time is your most valuable commodity. Time you spend on a low probability customer is time away from another customer with a higher probability of an order. Pay attention to those customers that you are better suited to serve their needs, you have a product that is proven to be right for them, and you can be competitive. Don't forget customers that you are on good terms with, and who seem to like you. This focus will increase your chances of getting sales.

Every interaction with a customer gives you an opportunity to gauge reactions and to soak up the general feel of your dealings with them. As you get to know the individuals you do business with, the better you will start picking up on when they are happy, irritated, or outright mad. It doesn't always show on the outside, but the words that are chosen and the tone used are a dead giveaway if you take a moment to analyze them. It's important to revisit what was said in a meeting, on a phone call, or in an email because it's easy to miss certain cues when you are busy in that moment concentrating on dates, specifications, pricing, etc. A second look can reveal an underlying tone you missed the first time around.

A lot of salespeople put on their rose colored glasses when they talk to a customer. They are so intent on making a sale that even when they are given all the clues to make a thorough analysis of the situation, they are either incapable of making an objective evaluation or are so concentrated on their own agenda they completely miss the cues, or refuse to see them. More about objectivity in the next section.

At all times during the sales process, keep in mind what the customer wants and how you are meeting their needs. Communication is the key. Don't just wait in the office for the phone to ring or email to bling. Sales, as a whole, should be considered a liquid trade where needs can quickly change, and you need to respond to those changes quickly and proficiently. Look for the signs of change. Be proactive if you don't want to be left behind.

As customers move through the quotation process, they become more educated about available products on the market and constantly re-evaluate their options. Especially with large purchases, it is likely that the customer will modify their requirements several times before placing an order. This is why constant communication is so important. You don't want to be quoting a version of specifications that is several weeks old while the customer moves on with other bidders that are current.

## Front Runners: A Lesson in Real Life Selling

Every time a customer makes a drastic change in their requirements there is a reason for it; a trigger. You need to know and recognize that trigger. This impulse could have come from the customer's own organization, or from one of your competitors. Your competitor has convinced them that this new specification is somehow better for them (the customer) than the old specification. It is probably better for your competitor too because every salesperson is trying to quote an item where they have technical, delivery, or cost advantages. This can change the front runner among the bidders. If you were the previous front runner, you are now chasing the other guy.

Here is information that many salespeople go through their entire career without knowing: in the above situation, you know you are not the front runner bidder because the customer did not inform you first that they were thinking of changing the specifications for the quote request. The customer will almost always check with the front runner before they make changes to their specification, and will use the front runner as a sounding board. The front runner is the front runner because the customer prefers them (at this time). If the front runner has good reasons to not change the specification, the customer will, most likely, not change it.

> I had a customer that had been placing repeat orders to us for several years. It was an excellent relationship. They were looking for an item that they knew we didn't really make or offer. They came to me, gave me a copy of another supplier's quote for the item, and told me if I could match the price they would become our first reference customer for the item. They said they understood it would take longer for us to design and manufacture the item since we had not done it before, but it was ok. We were, and stayed, the front runner

based on our past performance and the high level of trust that had been established in the customer relationship.

A client of mine sells security products. Recently, he quoted his biggest prospect yet. The customer had never bought from the company before, but told the salesperson if he could provide a good price, he would place an order. The salesperson put the quote together, squeezed the margin to below average, and sent it out on a Friday morning. At 4:00pm, he called the customer to follow up, but was told that his contact had left for the weekend. Had he really, or did he just not want to talk? On Monday morning the salesperson received an email that said a competitor, the customer's long time security products supplier, had beaten the price by $1000. Most likely the competitor was the front runner supplier, and the customer had provided them with the quote and asked if they could match it. In other words, this salesperson never really had a chance.

So, what are you supposed to do when you worked so hard preparing that material and the decision was already practically made before you even sent the quote to the customer? Was it all for nothing? First of all, you shake off your feelings of anger and disappointment. This is the reality of a sales career. The customer owes you nothing. You continue to send quotes to the customer and wait for the moment when the front runner disappoints them or can't meet their need – because eventually it will happen – and you will be primed and ready to take their place.

## Be Objective in Your Analysis

It is difficult to be objective when analyzing a customer, and especially yourself. After all, you have a lot riding on the relationship. You want to make a sale, and it's a lot nicer to turn a blind eye to all the cues and just believe that everything is going great and there's an order in the pipeline. However, if you are ever going to become a great salesperson, you need to be objective. The information you gather and produce must be reliable and useful. Jumping to the conclusion that you did everything right and the customer did everything wrong whenever a quote doesn't go your way may indicate that you are not making an honest, unbiased analysis of the situation. Of course, it is possible that you did do everything right, but even so, did every customer every time do absolutely everything wrong?

Analyzing when or how you went wrong is not pleasant. It certainly is much easier, though, than having someone else do it; then, publicly sharing their conclusions and opinions with other people. This is what customers do if they are not happy with your work. So get to it.

Break a sale into its six individual components to see where it went right or wrong:

1. Customer needs
2. The match between your offer and the customer's needs
3. Price
4. Delivery time
5. Your feelings about the customer. How were they when they dealt with you? Were you a front runner, or not?
6. How wide a base of contacts did you create throughout the customer's organization? (Width and depth is discussed in Chapter 12)

You will not have all the factual data, and will have to rely on your gut feeling for some parts. As you deal more with this customer, you will develop additional information as well as learn their style. And, as you collect more information, your analysis becomes more effective. This is why salespeople do better with existing customers versus new ones. If you keep doing this for a while, you will develop a process and your analytical skills will grow more reliable.

Performing this analysis when you lose an order provides useful information moving forward; and hopefully, it helps you find closure so you can quit thinking about it and move on to the next quote.

## Get a Second Opinion

There will be cases when you feel plain old stuck. You feel like you haven't taken the right approach, and just cannot seem to figure out a way forward. Maybe there's a personality clash.

In these cases, it is really helpful to have your manager or a trusted coworker who you can ask to evaluate the situation. Give this other person all the facts and your observations, and have them formulate a second opinion for you. This opinion may be related to pricing, the technical solution, or just about any other part of the process (think the six individual sales components above). It may even be about how to deal with the personalities involved. Hopefully, having a second set of eyes to look at the material and discuss it will help you come up with an idea you did not think of on your own.

In return, maybe you can help your coworker in a similar situation; thus, creating a bilateral working relationship beneficial for both parties.

## Utilize Your Organization

Sales can feel like solitary work; an individual sport to be played on your own. What you have to keep in mind is that unless you are a small business entrepreneur, there is an entire organization behind you. Within that organization are knowledgeable people who can answer your questions. If you can tap into that experience and wisdom, you will be way ahead in the game versus trying to learn on your own and repeating the mistakes made by the people before you. But if you do not ask, it is impossible for others to know that you need help.

If you are truly working by yourself, like someone such as an entrepreneur or small business owner, I would suggest you find another person you can use as a sounding board for ideas and discussion, and offer them the same in return. It can be very fruitful. If you can't find someone you trust, get in touch with us.

Be respectful of your coworkers. You don't have to be everyone's best friend, but don't be a time hog either. If someone takes the time to help you, be appreciative. Understand that they are trying to get ahead too, and, just like you, time is their most valuable resource. Make helping you worth their while by offering them help when you can. A give and take relationship is always the best.

If you tried this before and it ended as a more give–give on your part, don't hold a grudge. The next person might be a great help.

## Momentum Can Change on a Dime

As you are working diligently through the sales process with a customer, so are all your competitors. One minute you're the front runner bidder, and the next you're not. Or, it can be the other way around. Most times, you don't even know what happened or when exactly it happened. Sometimes your gut tells you something went horribly wrong.

> I was working with a new software product, and targeted a company in California that developed large enterprise resource planning software. We were hoping to be an add-on module in their product. I visited them, and we created a demo platform where we hooked both software programs together to create a live testing environment to move data back and forth. I'll spare you the details, but

> the testing went horribly wrong. Our software did not do what we claimed it would. Up to that point, we had a good chance of developing a business relationship with this company. After the testing, we were deemed completely untrustworthy. We never got a second chance. We were done and out.

And then, sometimes everything goes incredibly right.

> I was selling the very same software when I was invited to a company that works on nuclear power plants. The company was a startup with lots of venture capital. I went to visit them and gave a product presentation. The company president and two managers attended the meeting. The presentation went very well. We downloaded some of their data into our software, and it worked flawlessly. Afterwards during dinner, the president stood up, stuck out his hand and said, "We have decided we will order from you." I thought it was just a product presentation and the order wouldn't be placed for a long time, but it wasn't worth it for them to take time evaluating other alternatives when they were convinced our product would do the job.

So, what are the signs of changing momentum? Typically, you should start worrying when a customer does not answer your voice mails or emails with the same tone or frequency they used to. A clear symptom of this is when the customer stops giving you advice on how you should modify your quotation in order to be more competitive. They don't initiate contact anymore, even though before they were calling all the time with questions. There are no requests for clarifications, no modifications on the scope of supply or the delivery schedule; nothing. They haven't set up a time to meet with you or discuss the quote over the phone. When you call to push a meeting, the answer is often, "I'm too busy," or "Let's do it later." They don't return your calls in a timely fashion. When you do get them on the phone, they don't have time to talk to you; they are late for a meeting. Keep in mind that throughout all of this they continue to be polite, which is often misread by the salesperson as a positive sign.

The opposite is true if you suddenly become the front runner bidder. The customer starts calling you all the time, they pay attention to what you are saying, they ask specific questions, and want to know more about the benefits of your product over others. This behavior helps the customer reinforce the idea that they are making the right decision.

Even if the customer does not intend to let you know there has been a change in the front runner bidder, it is impossible for it to not show and to have an impact on their behavior. It always shows one way or another if you know what signs to look for.

Your main task as the quotation leader is to make sure there are zero doubts on the customer's side that could prevent them from ordering from you. It's important to be aware at all times that a customer can change their mind at any moment; you have to be cautious and observant when dealing with both existing customers and potential customers.

# 15.

# CUSTOMER CONTACT: HOW OFTEN?

*How often should I contact a customer?* is one of the most commonly asked questions during sales training. Unfortunately, there are no set times for exactly when or how often you should talk to a customer. It depends. (Yes, I know. I hate those answers too.) Although there are no set guidelines, there are some good rules of thumb regarding customer contact. They are covered in the sections below.

The most basic rule is to keep in touch often enough to make sure the customer remembers you and your company every time they order a product or service that you can provide. If you get the feeling that is has been too long since the customer heard from you in one form or another (phone, email, text, mailing), it may be time to do something about it. Just keep in mind there is a fine line between frequent contact and being a pest. If you are contacting them too often, you might be irritating them and ruining a chance for creating a good relationship.

Never rely on email alone to communicate with customers. It is too easy to misunderstand words and sentences, and unanswered emails may be interpreted negatively if they are not answered right away. Every person has their own idea of what is an acceptable time period to answer an email. Communication based on emails or text messages is distant, and can appear cold or uncaring. It also makes it difficult to receive immediate and important feedback like the enthusiastic "Great!" or the not so enthusiastic "Oh." Phone calls are important, and visits even more important. Do not underestimate the power of human contact over electronic contact. When taking a long term perspective, a visit to a customer is rarely a waste of time. Body language and tone of voice are significant parts of communication. During a visit you get the whole package, on the phone you get most of it, by using email or text communication you completely lose this part of the message.

## Calling Small Businesses versus Calling Bigger Businesses

> Note:
> Salespeople often use the following recipe for communication:
>
> All good news, you call
> All bad news, you call
> For anything in between, you can use email

Some of your customers could very well be small businesses, maybe even one man operations. (This does not diminish their importance as a customer.) When you call, you often get the owner on the phone. At times they may appear abrupt, and don't want to chit chat. Before getting offended or ignoring it altogether, you have to understand that time is money for the small business owner. If it is a roofing company and they have to finish a roof by the end of the day so they can get paid and move on to the next job, they probably just don't have a lot of spare time to spend on sales calls. Especially if they don't have an immediate need for your product. Respect their time and make your point quickly; then, get off the phone. Send a confirmation email afterwards. They will appreciate it a lot more than the salesperson who tries to hang on the line as long as possible in the desperate hope they will sell something. Save yourself time; take no for an answer this time and move on to the next customer.

Big businesses are a different story. The reception you receive can be mixed. Some folks won't even take your call while others will stay on the phone as long as you want. Years ago, I had a work mate who spent hours talking to salespeople on the phone. He asked questions about product applications, installation, limitations, the weather. He had them come in and make product presentations to him. After all, it wasn't his time and money. On the flip side, I've dealt with secretaries that make breaking into Fort Knox look easy.

Getting through a good secretary or assistant is tough, but possible. You must understand that they are trying to do their job. It's very possible they've been specifically instructed to keep salespeople like you out. Over time you will develop a relationship with this gate keeper, and there will be a time when they will help you. First, you have to convince them of the merits of letting you speak to their boss. Never snub them because you feel they are *only a secretary*. That will guarantee your failure for sure. They may not have a big title, but they can have an unbelievable amount of indirect power, and they aren't afraid of using it.

## One Time Customer versus the Repeat Customer

There are items like gas and food that we buy on a weekly basis, and every week we end up at the same stores. We don't even try to get multiple bids, or write a contract for these items outside of a sales receipt because we don't really consider ourselves buying anything. We're just getting something, or picking up something. The general opinion around items like these is that there is not that much difference in price or quality between the places we go and another one. We choose the places we do because of convenience or habit, and tend to stay with the same provider.

The same is pretty much true for companies. They tend to keep using the same supplier for items that are considered, in their scale, low value. (Low value means something different for every company: from the one person business to a Fortune 500 company.) Price level bids might be accepted and evaluated once per year, and then the winner gets the business for the next period. There's not enough to be saved to make it worth spending a lot of time finding new suppliers. There is not enough payback for the expenses incurred.

Regardless of the business, a certain portion of customers are repeat customers or regulars, and the remaining customers are either one time customers or infrequent customers. Regular customers are great. For one reason or another they have decided that you fill their needs, and as long as they don't find a reason to take their business elsewhere you are all set. You can even ignore these customers to some extent because the relationship has already been established, and they trust that their needs are taken care of. They will also give you a bit more latitude if issues out of the ordinary arise.

One time and infrequent customers require a lot more selling to convert them into regulars. They may be regulars of another company, but for some reason – no capacity, vacation, or any other abnormal situation – they are looking to buy items from somewhere else. Your job is to find the trigger that will make them start using you as their main supplier. You need to be faster than their current supplier, or cheaper, or friendlier, whatever it takes to woo them over to your business. They can't be ignored and need extra attention. You want them to think, *How come my current supplier doesn't do this?* Since they keep coming back every now and then, it might be productive to strike a business development conversation with them. Be direct; ask them where they usually do business. What would you have to do to get them to become your regular customer? Even if they aren't convinced, because most likely they will stay with their current supplier until given a reason not to, it is your duty to at least try and convert them. If you do this tactfully, they may actually like that you tried. At minimum, it gives you a perfect opportunity to collect market data on your competitor. These customers need a bit more customer contact every time they do business with you. One reason is for them to get to know you better.

## Weekly or Biweekly Contact

If a customer is in contact with you every week or at least once every two weeks, you rarely need to make additional marketing or contact calls. They know you, you are bidding on their items, and they are buying from you too. If you start calling in between to see how they are doing or to ask if there is anything else you can help them with, you run the danger of irritating them. They are not going to appreciate you trying to initiate extra communication when you are in regular contact already.

You can still start rolling out this customer. When you have them on the phone discussing the bid requests you are receiving, ask if there are any other products or services they are buying from someone else and tell them that you would be interested in bidding on them as well. Most people don't mind if you ask them directly, instead of beating around the bush and trying to be clever about it. "Mike, while I have you on the phone I have a question. Since you are buying our XXX, you most likely need HHH, as well. Would you mind telling me who you buy them from and if I can bid on them next time you need them?" He always has the opportunity to say, "No, you may not because of YYY." However, without bringing it to his attention he may not even know that you can supply that item too.

If this customer tells you they are bidding on a big job that will be decided in a month or two, it is ok to ask them in three to four weeks if it has materialized yet.

You can also ask if they have any other people who are purchasing and placing product orders. If you are polite, direct, and take no for an answer if it is given; then, asking for additional contacts should not weaken your current relationship. You always have to keep in mind that even if you get a no today and you are respectful of that decision, two months from now, after your relationship with the customer has solidified or they aren't happy with the current supplier, you may get a yes. It's different if you refuse to take no for an answer and insist upon getting what you want. That situation could clearly damage your current or long term relationship.

You've hit the jackpot if the company has other locations in your territory. Ask for the contact in another location and permission to use your customer's name in the introduction. Then, you simply call them.

"My name is Sue from XXX. We are currently supplying FFF to your facility in DDD. My contact person there is Mike JJJ. I see we aren't currently doing any business with your location. How can I start the process of getting requests from your location too?"

These customers are your absolute best case scenarios to grow. They already have an account, are familiar with you and your company, and obviously trust you as a supplier. Keep files on these customers like organizational charts, and update the information as you learn more. Often people move within a company to another location, and if a person who favored your product or service moves to another location, there is a good chance they can get you "in."

## Monthly Contact

Customers you are dealing with on a monthly basis are still relatively easy. The four to six week time period is short enough for them to remember your name and voice.

Be aware that other suppliers are calling these customers too. Make sure that you do keep in touch, and when the opportunity for a meeting arises you are there. I was once told by a buyer at a large steel mill in North America that he receives up to 100 calls per week from potential suppliers asking for a meeting. Be appreciative of how difficult it really is to get that meeting, and when you get it don't blow it.

Here, a rule of thumb is if you haven't heard from your customer in six weeks, give them a call. The time is a bit longer, so you can inquire as to how they are doing and if they see any need for your offerings in the near future. Often, after a call like this you will see some sort of quote request coming your way. They may have simply forgotten you. Another plausible alternative is that following the phone call, they went through their desk and found something that they needed and figured they might as well send it to you. Be happy you called and reminded them.

If you call and there is nothing pertinent going on, you can end the phone call by asking them if you have not heard from them if it's ok to give them a call in four to six weeks. If the time frame is pushed that far out, how can anyone say no? They will most likely say "sure." Mark it in your calendar to give them a call around four to five weeks from now.

## Quarterly or Yearly Contact

Keeping a relationship with these customers is challenging.

> Let's say that you sell real estate, and you just sold a customer a house. This means that the customer is probably out of the market for a period of time. The question is, for how long? Some people live in one house for 30 years, and others buy another house in less than two years. This is the reason why your realtor sends you their calendar, card, or some other communication at least once per year. Many of them send marketing material even more often than that. They are also happy to include your name on their daily or weekly automated email of new listings. They consider you *their* customer, and are terrified that the day you decide to list your house you might not remember them and list your house with someone else. They also want to keep themselves fresh in your mind in case a friend asks you for the name of a good realtor in the area.

The same issues come into play if you sell big ticket items or capital equipment. If you sell solar systems, you are almost even worse off. If a customer's roof has been filled with panels, what do you sell them next? They are pretty much off the market until they move to another house, or technology advances to a point where you can convince them to upgrade the system, at which time they could be customers again.

It's a difficult question. How often should you be in contact with these customers? There really is no good cut and dried answer that I can think of, but I would say absolutely no less than once or twice per year. I am a believer that a short phone call twice per year is more effective than ten emails. I have tried different methods over the years, and what ends up happening is that salespeople do the best they can and randomly keep in touch. These customers do not realistically expect anyone to call or visit them every month, or even every quarter. Nevertheless, as far as the salesperson is concerned, the target is still unchanged. When this customer starts looking at a product or service the salesperson's company can supply, they want the customer to remember their name and their company.

If you are working with long sales cycle items and you do not have anything urgent going on with a customer, you can contact them once per quarter or a couple times per year. The idea here is to just say a quick hello and let them know you called to see how they were doing. What you are saying in between the lines is that, "I am still here ready and willing to serve you as soon as you get a need."

# PART VI:
# MANAGING A SALES FORCE

# 16.

# MEASURING AND REPORTING SALES SUCCESS: KEY PEFORMANCE INDICATORS

As I've mentioned earlier, you get what you measure. And this is why you have to be careful about what you set out to measure, especially in sales. There are numerous key performance indicators (KPI's) within the average company's sales department for measuring everything from gross sales to number of phone calls made.

Companies develop KPI's for tracking and comparing their sales force. Indicators are measured on a weekly or monthly basis. Many companies internally publish these KPI's for each individual salesperson. Knowing where they stand in comparison to their peers can act as a strong motivator. The unwritten goal is to get poor performers to pick up their pace.

Measuring and reporting success related to sales is difficult because there are a number of factors outside the control of the individual salesperson, such as the size and quality of a territory. In products like cars, vitamins, and mattresses the comparison between salespeople is easier because the product pricing does not vary dramatically from salesperson to salesperson. Nevertheless, there is a big difference in product demand between various work schedules. Saturday is a better shift to work than Tuesday for the car salesperson.

It's more challenging in the field of BTO (built-to-order), ETO (engineered-to-order), and any other project type sales where goods are highly customized because the sales cycle from initial contact to contract signing can be several years. A lot of things happen during this time.

In BTO and ETO businesses each sale, each customer, and each project are different. The real results – was a project profitable and if so, how much – are evident only after the product has been delivered and the sales project closed. Again, many factors that play into the final success of a sale are out of the control of the salesperson. For example: purchasing, subcontractor schedules, inventory levels at subcontractors or suppliers, design quality, and vacations.

> I recently ran into a project manager of a large power generation equipment supplier at the airport. He was flying home from a customer meeting. The customer had issues with equipment his company had delivered. He found that during the manufacturing process, a small metal burr was left in one of the machined pipes. It held for several weeks after startup; then, one day it let loose and was pushed through the system by high pressure. The equipment came to a grinding halt, and power generation stopped. The customer called the supplier's sales department because that's who they know best. They demanded the problem be fixed immediately. They stressed how they had chosen the supplier because they felt they could trust them, but if their problem wasn't remedied right now they would start buying their equipment from someone else. I imagine they named one or two of the supplier's top competitors to give more impact. The head of sales at the supplier's company called the head of projects, emphasizing the importance of *this* customer. The head of projects called his project manager and told him that the issue needed to be fixed immediately.

What if there are no parts in inventory to immediately repair the equipment? What if the salesperson, that is different from the project manager, loses the next order because of how this issue was handled? Is it the salesperson's fault? Should the salesperson have been able to predict the future, and price this blip into the original cost? How could it have been avoided?

Companies try to simplify the process of sales personnel measurement by tracking only gross sales or sales margin per sales manager, but this is not enough. Neither is percentage of profit nor absolute profit numbers alone an adequate measurement of success. More information is required for a real business analysis. Surprisingly in some cases, the big seller in the sales force that is taking unknown risks or intentionally downplaying the known risks, is actually less profitable for the company than the salesperson who sells less, but more cautiously. There is a joke among small business owners fighting for a very large order that, "This order is big enough to put the entire company out of business."

> According to a *World at Work* Survey (2012), over 80% of budgets are based on the previous year's results.

You will know what I mean by the end of this chapter.

## The Effects of Different Measures on Sales Performance: A Case Study

This case study demonstrates how easily evaluations of salespeople can change when data is added to a performance analysis.

Company A has six sales managers. The company's sales budget for the fiscal year is $23.4 million. Each sales manager has a varying amount of experience, diverse product lines, and different sized and quality territories. Individual sales budgets have been set in the following way: Ed's budget is $6,500; Jack's is $6,000; Morty's is $5,000; Otto's is

# 176  SALES INTELLIGENCE

$3,500; Mike's is $2,000; and Mary's is $400. (All dollars are expressed in thousands.)

Yearend sales results are reported in the chart below. Total company sales were less than budgeted: $20.0 million, about 15% below budget.

| Name | Sales Budget | Actual Gross Sales | % of Budget |
|---|---|---|---|
| Ed | 6,500 | 5,000 | 77% |
| Jack | 6,000 | 4,500 | 75% |
| Morty | 5,000 | 4,400 | 88% |
| Otto | 3,500 | 3,700 | 106% |
| Mike | 2,000 | 2,500 | 125% |
| Mary | 400 | 400 | 100% |

The first thoughts that come to mind:

- Should all the sales managers be measured against this reduced scale?
- How were individual sales manager's budgets determined?
- Does this company have a bonus system?
- The difference between the biggest and smallest budget seems awfully large (15x).
- What is the difference in the typical customer order between Mary and Ed?
- If one manager exceeded budget, but the company as a whole did not reach the budget, is their performance more impressive than the others who fell below?
- Should the numbers be adjusted for different product lines based on demand?

Ed sold $5,000 and Mike sold $2,500. Ed clearly fell below his budget, and Mike clearly sold above his budget if the company's main KPI is gross sales. Should Mike be rewarded with a nice bonus, and Ed reprimanded and told he really has to pick up the pace? However, in absolute numbers Ed sold twice the amount Mike sold. And, even though Ed is below budget, he still sold more than any other sales manager, so how bad of a sales guy can Ed really be? It doesn't seem fair to Ed, does it?

Does the company even need Mary? Her budget was approximately one-sixteenth of Ed's. She reached her quota, but with numbers that small how can she not? Right? According to these numbers, the company needs 12 Marys to make up for one Ed. Is Mary just plain old lazy and not interested in working hard? Since Morty sold 11 times what Mary sold, should he get 11 times Mary's pay too?

> How do we ensure that all these sales managers are working to their fullest capacity? How do we compensate them fairly for their work?

Gross profit margins are added for each sales manager in the table below:

| Name | Sales Budget | Actual Gross Sales | % of Budget | Gross Profit % |
|------|--------------|--------------------|-------------|----------------|
| Ed   | 6,500        | 5,000              | 77%         | 24%            |
| Jack | 6,000        | 4,500              | 75%         | 26%            |
| Morty| 5,000        | 4,400              | 88%         | 18%            |
| Otto | 3,500        | 3,700              | 106%        | 34%            |
| Mike | 2,000        | 2,500              | 125%        | 14%            |
| Mary | 400          | 400                | 100%        | 45%            |

What do the gross profit margin percentages tell us? They seem to imply that out of nowhere, Otto is the best performing sales manager. He sold more than budget (106%), and his profit margin is second only to Mary. But, what if the company KPI's do not account for a combination of several components?

Mike exceeded his gross sales, but failed miserably in profit margin when compared to the others; however, the company still made money. Mike points out that his product line has the toughest competition and without his skills (i.e. anyone else selling this product) the margins would have been much worse. Otto thinks that Mike lowered the profit margins just to sell more and make his bonus. In Otto's opinion, Mike cheated because everyone else tried to hold onto the agreed profit margin. Meanwhile, Mary tells everyone in the office how no one else even comes close to her sales ability. After all, she's selling at a profit margin almost double the others' numbers. In her opinion, Mike is giving product away, and only she and Otto should get the performance bonus. Mike responds that his top $400k in sales are at 39% profit margin; the total amount of Mary's budget. He also sold an *additional* $2.1 million. "Where's your $2.1 million in sales, Mary?" he asks.

Next, absolute profit dollars are added to the performance results.

| Name | Sales Budget | Actual Gross Sales | % of Budget | Gross Profit % | Gross Profit |
|---|---|---|---|---|---|
| Ed | 6,500 | 5,000 | 77% | 24% | 1,200 |
| Jack | 6,000 | 4,500 | 75% | 26% | 1,170 |
| Morty | 5,000 | 4,400 | 88% | 18% | 810 |
| Otto | 3,500 | 3,700 | 106% | 34% | 1,224 |
| Mike | 2,000 | 2,500 | 125% | 14% | 350 |
| Mary | 400 | 400 | 100% | 45% | 180 |

Ok, so now we look at the gross profit in absolute dollars. Ed, Jack, and Otto have each brought in over a million dollars in profits. "Say what you want, but there are only three of us bringing in over a million dollars in profits," says Jack. Ed chimes in, "Hats off to you, Otto. Who cares if Jack and I fell slightly below the budget in gross sales? Without the three of us, the company would not be here." Mike is of the opinion that anyone meeting or exceeding their gross sales quota should get a bonus,

## MEASURING AND REPORTING SALES SUCCESS 179

regardless of how the company did as a whole because "We all had a gross sales budget as our target, everyone knew it, and everyone had the same chance of hitting that target."

Who are the real stars of this sales organization? Let's go back to the original question. Based on the scenario above, who is rewarded? How, and based on what? What metrics justify rewards? Which indicators will produce an equitable measurement that every sales manager can appreciate and accept as a fair system, so they will work as a team supporting each other to produce maximum results for the company?

> According to a 2012 *World at Work* survey of 2011 sales compensation plan payouts, only 18% of respondents agreed that payouts were *fully* aligned with results.

The next addition to the chart is where fixed costs are deducted to get a net profit and net profit percentage. At the budgeted $23.4 million in sales, overhead and interest costs were originally calculated when budgets were made at $3.22 million, or about 14% of turnover. Due to lower than predicted sales, the actual yearend overhead and interest cost came in at $3.22 million, but due to lower sales figures the percentage ended at 16%.

| Name | Sales Budget | Actual Gross Sales | % of Budget | Gross Profit % | Gross Profit | Net Profit | Net Profit % |
|---|---|---|---|---|---|---|---|
| Ed | 6,500 | 5,000 | 77% | 24% | 1,200 | 400 | 8% |
| Jack | 6,000 | 4,500 | 75% | 26% | 1,170 | 440 | 10% |
| Morty | 5,000 | 4,400 | 88% | 18% | 810 | 90 | 2% |
| Otto | 3,500 | 3,700 | 106% | 34% | 1,224 | 648 | 18% |
| Mike | 2,000 | 2,500 | 125% | 14% | 350 | -50 | -2% |
| Mary | 400 | 400 | 100% | 45% | 180 | 116 | 29% |

180   SALES INTELLIGENCE

What's up with Mike now? His projects actually lost money! But, his earlier numbers looked so good. "I do not understand this," says his sales director. Mike is convinced that if he didn't bring in the $2.5 million in sales, fixed costs would reduce everyone's profit because total company sales would have been less. And, if everyone else exceeded their sales budget by over 20% like he did, his projects would not have lost any money. A quick glance confirms that now Ed, Jack, and Otto are the ones keeping the company alive. Mary may not be the biggest seller, but at least she is bringing in money. Something has to be done about Mike, but then again, according to his gross sales (the only company KPI was gross sales compared to budget) he actually earned a bonus for this year.

It's enough to make the VP of sales' head spin. *This is way too difficult*, he thinks. *Maybe I'll just tell everyone that because as a company we did not meet our goals, we will not reward anyone."* The CFO agrees with this plan (of course he does). After all, neither the department nor the company as a whole met its goal.

Now, we'll add one more table. This time sales managers' performance is measured after projects are delivered, the 1 year warranty period is fulfilled, and sales projects are closed.

| Name | Sales Budget | Actual Gross Sales | % of Budget | Gross Profit % | Gross Profit | Net Result | Net Profit % |
|---|---|---|---|---|---|---|---|
| Ed | 6,500 | 5,000 | 77% | 24% | 1,200 | 278 | 6% |
| Jack | 6,000 | 4,500 | 75% | 26% | 1,170 | 390 | 9% |
| Morty | 5,000 | 4,400 | 88% | 18% | 810 | -550 | -13% |
| Otto | 3,500 | 3,700 | 106% | 34% | 1,224 | 417 | 11% |
| Mike | 2,000 | 2,500 | 125% | 14% | 350 | 0 | 0% |
| Mary | 400 | 400 | 100% | 45% | 180 | 135 | 34% |

Again, adding more data changes the results. It looks like the more

Morty sells, the more money the company loses. How can his projects lose so much money? Are all of his projects losing money, or just one? What other variables are there to look at? Is Morty just a sloppy sales manager, or do we have project management issues? Mike's projects were losing money based on the other data, but actually they are not. However, they aren't making money either. Mary's projects are still producing great profit margins.

The deeper you dig the more you find, and the muddier the big picture gets. Making judgments based solely on one number in this, or any other business is dangerous.

Key performance indicators should be designed very carefully. As illustrated above, adding indicators to a performance analysis yields dramatically different results. If Gross Sales is the only measure of success at the end of the year, Mike is the top sales performer at Company A. When other KPI's are implemented Mike falls to the bottom of the pack, and the top positions go to Otto and Mary. But, what do we do with Morty?

I'll go back to my original question one more time. How would you reward the salespeople in the above Company A for their performance? It's not so easy to answer, is it? Yet, more than not, companies are basing compensation strictly on gross sales or margins. Remember the survey in the text box above. Only 18% of respondents thought that payouts were fully aligned with results. A wrong, or one-sided method can promote risk taking, sloppy or inaccurate cost calculations, reduce or completely eliminate assisting or training of new sales personnel (Why bother?), and over time create a sales force that operates in cut-throat ways toward each other. The list goes on and on.

When part of a salesperson's compensation is tied to margins only, it's supposed to incite the salesperson to sell at higher margins, but sometimes the opposite happens. If there is a threshold of gross profit that each sales manager should, at minimum, produce, there is a great danger of sub-optimization. Furthermore, it is extremely difficult to get an approval of these schemes from your troops. I'd say the most important feature of any sales commission plan is that it has to be fair to everyone. Otherwise, it can cause more bitterness than goodwill.

Performance rewards that are communicated poorly or misunderstood by the troops can demotivate a sales team, even if the principles are sound. Concepts need to be introduced and explained properly, so the sales team can justify them in their minds. It's also important to understand that including certain KPI's in the reward system will make salespeople perform differently. Targeting high margins implies selling at higher prices, which in turn can lead to fewer sales. Setting gross sales as the performance measure can mean higher sales at the cost of lower profit margins.

## The Relationship With Your Manager

Everyone has good days and bad days. It's just a fact of life that sometimes you love your job, and sometimes you would rather have a root canal than clock in at the office. The important issue, though, is how you conduct yourself.

When you are frustrated, tired, or in a bad mood and your manager says something that irritates you, your natural inclination may be to start gossiping with a coworker. *Your boss is a blockhead and you could do his job ten times better.* You tell your gripe to one person in confidence; then, they repeat it to a third person, but don't stress the confidence factor quite so much because they are not a stakeholder in the outcome if it gets out, and so on. Eventually, the word reaches the ears of your manager. Take my advice: just keep your thoughts to yourself and your mouth shut.

Think about the people you work with now. If you were the manager, how would you perceive them? Would you hand over the company's most important accounts to the complainer? Would you fire the best performing salesperson on the team because you believe he only makes sales because he's such a royal butt kisser? Would you (as a manager) think you (as a salesperson) are hard working or a slacker? Why or why not? If you want to get ahead in your career, it's good practice to start thinking about these things outside the realm of your own emotions. Stop being jealous or judgmental of others, and focus that energy on your own end game. I promise it will be time well spent.

Keep your manager involved. Let them know what you are doing. Give them the tools to support you. You help them; they help you. That's the way it works. Your days will go by much faster, and you will be better regarded by everyone. Maybe the next promotion, or the one after, will be yours. If not, it's still important to create good references.

It took me years and the actual rise to a CEO position to realize that bosses are not asses because they want to be. They are answering to managers too – the CEO answers to the board of directors and investors. The usual culprit, though, is communication between the levels of an organization can be misinterpreted, and conclusions are drawn without asking for clarification.

## Enthusiasm or Experience

When customers express interest in a company's products or services in the form of quotation requests, how should those quotation requests be divided among salespeople, and how is it typically done? In my experience, a company obtains quote requests in four ways:

1. A salesperson finds a potential customer
2. A salesperson is contacted by a customer
3. The company receives a general request that is passed on to a salesperson or the head of sales

4. A customer asks another employee of a company to spread the word that they would like to speak with a salesperson

Depending on how the company is set up, the request may go to a point person who divides the work in a similar way tables at a restaurant are divided up between wait staff by the hostess. This person may be the director of sales. If the customer already has an account manager; then, it will most likely be directed to that person. It's also possible that the person who receives the request is allowed to run with it. Whatever system is implemented, it is important that absolutely everyone in the department knows how, and based on what, requests are divided up.

In companies with no territories and where customers are not already divided between the salespeople, the point person often determines which sales manager gets which projects. This determination is based on numerous factors: the customer, the product requested, the magnitude of the potential order, salespeople's workload, the amount of work that the quote will require, and the schedule. The point person's aim is to allocate projects to the best suitable internal resources; namely, the salesperson that has the best chance of turning that request into an order. This is critical because again the intention is to make sales and not just quotations.

Enthusiastic hires with less experience sometimes misunderstand the situation, or feel that they are overlooked in this selection process. They have to understand that personal relationships with managers and customers will take time to build, but can be very rewarding when cultivated properly.

> A young sales manager once came to my corner office. He was frustrated with my sales director (and perhaps with his own performance). Outside of one or two small orders, he had not been able to make any sizeable sales during the past 16 months. I asked him why he thought

his results had been so modest. His neck turned beet red, "It's impossible for me to get sales due to the way this company's sales lead function is arranged." He explained how the director of sales took the juiciest RFQ's (Request for a Quotation) for himself to work on; then, divided the next best cases up among his best buddies – the old cronies. The only work left for the young guys was pure crap: the requests that customers asked for only to fulfill company requirements that purchasing obtain three bids before buying. It was obvious they would order from the same competitor they had been ordering from for years. "I didn't sign up for this. I want to get good prospects and make sales too. Unless I get better material to work with, expect the same results," he said.

I have to admit that partially he had a valid point. But, it also showed his immaturity and proved that he wasn't ready to be let loose on his own with our best customers. I told him that he had to have patience. The company divided up the work in much the same way that many other companies do it. The sales director couldn't afford to take chances with the best existing or biggest potential customers using recent hires that, due to inexperience, may make an expensive mistake during the process. That is why he, the self proclaimed *young gun*, got assigned the customers that, in his manager's opinion, were less likely to order. I told him that he had to just press on and do the best he could; with every quotation he was building a customer list of his own. Over time he would start seeing results. I also reminded him that his sales quota was very small due to this very reason.

As explained throughout this book, sales momentum can change on a dime. For that very reason, if territories are not carved out, customers and RFQ's with the highest potential are handled by the best and most experienced salespeople. If the company's sales are divided into territories or areas, there could be a significant difference in potential from one area to another. If you are a young gun and want to make it on that team of the best salespeople, keep in mind that this job is a marathon. One successful sale doesn't thrust you into the upper echelon; it takes repeated good performance. Keep at it, and over time your hard work will pay off.

## Overall Economy as a Factor in Sales

The economy affects all of us, but it affects some people really hard while others seem untouched. If unemployment goes up, it certainly affects those people who are unemployed or underemployed, but not so much the people who are still working the same as they were before.

It's the same for sales. If the overall economy is down, there will be less sales. And, competition for those dwindling sales opportunities is fierce. The opposite happens when the economy grows. There is an old saying: *the tide lifts all boats*. This is true to a certain extent, but is less true today than in the past. What tends to happen now is that those companies that are doing well to begin with will get more of the market share as the tide rises, and those companies that are not doing so well may temporarily keep their noses above water.

The economy can't be blamed every time your business sales are low because very rarely do sales drop to a solid zero. Keep in mind that if industry data shows it shrinking by 5%, it means that 95% of it is still out there. A lagging economy just means you must put more effort into getting the same amount of sales. Persistence is the name of the game. A positive spin on a tough situation is to remember that a prospect who is not ordering now, due to the economy or any other reason, may become a buying customer as the economy improves.

Just keep pounding on doors, making calls, and putting together those quotes because if you do not, it's guaranteed you won't make any sales.

# 17.

# SALES COMPENSATION

There is a lot of talk about salespeople's salaries. They are generally considered high, but according to the Bureau of Labor Statistics (BLS) numbers they are not as high as one might imagine. One reason these numbers may seem so low is that the BLS does a poor job dividing salespeople into sub-categories. Instead, they report on very broad categories. For example, a coffee shop barista is lumped in the same category as a real estate professional that is selling multi-million dollar properties in New York City. So, how are salespeople being compensated? Let's take a look.

There are a few different compensation plans for salespeople.

1. Straight competitive salary
2. Straight competitive salary plus commission
3. Low, below competitive salary plus commission
4. Pure commission

There are several components to consider when thinking about pay structure. More and more companies are pushing their salespeople to work as independent contractors using (4) and sometimes (3) to compensate them. Contractors can lose out on company bonuses, profit sharing, sick time, and other benefits.

> Jill sells medical equipment. She is offered two compensation packages by her employer. Estimated sales are $500,000/year.

a) Salary of $45,000/year + 3% Commission, which totals an income potential of $60,000/year.
b) A contract position that pays 18% Commission, which totals an income potential of $90,000/year.

Which package is better for Jill?

It may look like a no-brainer, but it is not. Jill needs to analyze the value of every component and then make a decision. In addition to the monetary value, this analysis should include non-monetary variables like Jill's comfort level with straight commission versus a guaranteed income, how she will cover sick time, and even her personality type. Is she a driven, self starter or does she prefer security?

## Sales Quota

It is important to know where quota numbers come from, and what data they are based on. Every salesperson should have a quota that is a bit labor intensive to reach, but not impossible.

> I once had a sales manager working for me who came up with the most ridiculous sales quotas. If he had sold $1 million the previous year, without the blink of an eye, he thought his quota for the following year should be $20 million. He reasoned that he had been working with his customers for a long time, and it was his turn to get the sale. That second year, he made sales between $3 million to $4 million. When the following year rolled around he suggested a budget of $25 million. An optimist looks like a pessimist after working with that guy. What if I were a VP of sales and I had ten people like this working for me? I could build a budget of $200 million just because my salespeople hoped to get that much. If they actually produced $20 million to $30 million sales that

year, I would have a big problem on my hands. I, for sure, would not see another budgeting year for that company.

This is the reason why budgets and quotas need to be carefully crafted.

I am not a big believer in the hard sale, and huge pressure on quotas and salespeople. The way I look at it is if someone works hard and the time is right, the results will come. If they don't, they don't. Pressuring and giving lip service to salespeople does not make their performance any better or faster. On the contrary, it may demotivate them. Of course, it's a different issue if I can see that the person is not working or is doing the wrong things.

# 18.

# CONTRACTS

Contracts are an important vehicle for both buyers and sellers to rely on during the final legs of the sales process. Whether you are selling bulk items or building a nuclear power plant; the scope, the process, the price, the schedule, the responsibilities, and the business cooperation must be agreed to in some way. Contracts are the most common way to communicate and make a record of this information.

Contracts can be negotiated before a supplier is chosen, or afterwards. It all depends on the company and the product or service they are buying. They can be one time contracts or ongoing contracts valid for a certain time period. Regardless of when the contract is prepared, both parties (supplier and buyer) have a high interest in keeping the other party interested in completing the process.

Most companies have their own standardized Terms and Conditions they like to follow. Fair warning: the typical customer's Terms and Conditions are bone chilling to read, so don't be surprised if it looks like they are impossible to fulfill, and mentally prepare yourself for it.

Contracts are all about foreseen and unforeseen risks. In tough races, the contract negotiations become a game of cat and mouse in the form of promises and responsibilities versus price and delivery time. Both parties are trying to make sure they are protected in the case of an unplanned event.

I have come across numerous salespeople that hate dealing with contracts, and because they hate them they want to stay as far away as possible from contract negotiations. This is a dangerous position to take because in the end it really does not matter what was discussed during a sale; what matters is what the contract states.

> I had a Sales Manager with several years of experience that I accompanied to Central Europe for contract negotiations at a customer. He was convinced that the customer had already decided to buy from us. The sales project had been going on for over a year, but we, as a potential supplier, had never received the customer's Terms & Conditions (T&C's). At the meeting the customer handed us their T&C's, and told us we had to sign them. Several alarms went off when I started reading the document. When I pointed out some of them, the customer got frustrated. They explained they were not authorized to negotiate the contract, and if there were some flags we would just have to price them into our quote. We did, and our price went up by 25%. The customer was surprised with the new price because they were expecting it to do down, not up. I explained that it was a direct result of the liability issues put forth in their T&C's. We were more than willing to negotiate a lower price if we could negotiate lower responsibility, as well. In the end, I could not accept the high risk of losing money on the project. We lost the order, and the sales manager was very upset with me. He went around the office telling people that, "Aijo did everything he could for us to not get the order."

This happened because the sales manager lost sight of the end goal. This happens easily to any sales manager when they are frustrated. They see the sale at hand, but the end goal is not to get a sale at any cost. The end goal is to make a *profitable* sale that takes into account the associated risks.

After this trip, I realized that my new sales force didn't really understand the importance of contracts. A contract is not something that is just haphazardly signed with the customer when everyone is feeling good, or something that is pushed off to the lawyers as a "not-my-job" kind of thing. A contract is a tool to make sure that each party understands what is expected of them, and the ramifications of not meeting those expectations. *Here is what you do, and this will happen if you don't do what you are promising to do.*

To remedy the situation, I implemented intensive contract training for all company salespeople where they were taught the potential pitfalls and the related costs associated with contract items. The bottom line here is that every sales manager must be interested in the contract so that they can price associated risk in it, and even more importantly they can start knocking those expensive clauses out as they move along. This way it does not come as a surprise during the final meeting. I understand that the sales manager is very eager at this point to get a sale, but someone in the company must be able to quantify the risks of that sale, make an objective evaluation regarding those risks, and carry the responsibility for that call.

Even if your company has a legal department or retains lawyers to draft contracts, you still need the skills to review what the customer requires from your company. I have noticed that since legal departments speak a different language than the technical and sales departments, they often concentrate on the obvious and completely miss the real risk that resides in the technical part of a sale. For example, if a contract item states that there is a delay penalty of 1% per week, the legal team contemplates whether it's 0.5% or 1%, when the real conversation should be centered around the definition and reasons of "delay."

To clarify this point, envision a contract that stipulates a customer requires building load data from a supplier 12 weeks after an order is placed, so they can purchase concrete piles. The very first thing the supplier should do is include an equivalent timeline of dates that specify when the customer needs to provide the supplier with the information necessary – such as soil type, topography, etc. – to calculate and produce the abovementioned data.

The real risk is not inherent in the 12 week number. The company engineers have done this many times before, and probably have a good rough estimate of how long it will take to complete. They can easily finish within the 12 week deadline. However, the time period becomes unclear – maybe impossible – if the customer doesn't provide the necessary data for them to do their job. Concentrating on a number of 12 weeks, 14 weeks, or even 9 weeks becomes moot.

> My company sold an automated process line to a meat processor. The original contract (I was not involved in the negotiations) stipulated that the line must pass 4,000 units per hour. What the contract did not specify was the dimension, weight, quality, or mix of the packages to reach this capacity. If packages are identified by barcode and barcodes can't be read, is that package counted toward the 4,000 or not if it is not clearly stated in the contract? What if the customer's production line cannot process 4,000 units per hour, and thus you can't prove that your equipment performs to contract capacity? If the contract clearly states that approval is based on showing and proving a capacity of 4,000 packages, how do you do it?

When the sales process reaches the point where talks are coming to a close and only a signature on the dotted line is needed, this is the 11th hour to take a time out and analyze all the risks involved. Any and all risks must be appropriately priced into a quotation. Higher risk, higher cost. Lower risk, lower cost. (There is nothing wrong with lower risk and higher cost if you can pull it off!)

## Legal Aspects of Sales

There is nothing illegal or unethical about either party in a contract negotiation trying to protect themselves to the extent that the other party allows it. Using legal jargon, there is a Latin saying – *Pacta Sunt Servanda* – which translates freely into something like "the contracts made must be followed." The law assumes that both parties that entered into the contract entered it willingly, and *understood* what exactly they entered into. Thus, you sign it and you follow it pretty much no matter what.

A bad contract or poorly understood contract negotiation can ruin a perfectly good sale, and instead of making a nice profit a project can become a money pit. Especially if the supplier doesn't understand the requirements, or in extreme cases did not even bother to read the contract to see in detail what was agreed. You might be thinking there is no way anyone is going to agree to a contract they did not read, but I would like to ask you this: when you created an account you use for social media did you read and understand the agreement, or did you just click Agree? It happens all the time. Contracts can be so unfriendly to read, partially by design, that people just give up and sign thinking that *it's probably all right*. Another popular thought process is, *why bring anything up when they aren't going to change it anyway?* The same fear exists in business. If you do not sign the contract presented to you by the customer, someone else might.

Today, contracts are even more important than in the past. It's the contract that often determines the financial outcome of a project. Oversights and misunderstandings cost money. Fair warning, there are customers out there who would like to slap a contractual ball and chain right on the supplier's leg. More often than not, these issues can be avoided if more attention is paid to the contract during negotiations.

I have often thought that a large contract is like a coin with two sides. One side has an image of what the seller sees they sold, and on the other side is an image of what the buyer thinks they purchased. Even if there is only one coin, the way both parties look at it can be quite different. The only two things that are crystal clear to both parties are cost and delivery time. The best way to minimize this discrepancy is to be clear in the contract. The better details are defined and consequences planned the better chance the project turns out well in the end.

During my first contract law class in the U.S., the professor kept saying, "You have to fight all your battles in contract negotiations, so you don't need to hire me later on in the process to defend you in the Court of Law." He was right!

> T&C's can be brutal. They are usually crafted by lawyers (not buyers) that have made an attempt to build in every conceivable event to protect their client, regardless of what happens.

## Drafting and Negotiating Contracts

Contracts are an essential part of the sales process. During larger sales, once potential suppliers have been shortlisted the customer's purchasing department gets involved in contract negotiations. Most large companies have their own Terms and Conditions (T&C's), and can be unwilling to make drastic changes to them. There are times when they won't accept any changes at all. It's important to realize that the customer's purchasing people, project managers, and legal personnel are very well versed in those T&C's, but the seller is often seeing them for the first time. Don't try to rush through. Take your time and make sure you understand it. The documents can be highly fragmented and cross referenced. One section refers to another, which in turn refers to a third one. It requires a lot of knowledge and patience to fully understand the entire document. Therefore, the supplier is at a definite disadvantage when the negotiations start. If you are the one representing a sale, you absolutely have to give contract negotiations the time and respect it deserves.

If a customer is totally unwilling to make any changes to the T&C's at all and answers your requests for changes in wording like, "add it into your price," you can safely assume you are not the front runner in the deal at that time. The customer's intention is not to pay more than necessary for items, and if you are offering to save them money by using different contract wording they should at least consider it. This is a valuable piece of information.

In large deals with multiple bidders, there are powerful dynamics at play. On one hand, the customer's organization is trying to rush to place an order with one of the suppliers. On the other hand, they also want each supplier to be very aware that there are several suppliers fighting for the order, and anyone can win. They want supplier's to feel pressured into accepting their terms and conditions. It is not a reason to take on unwarranted risk.

Based on information collected during the bidding phase, the customer's buying team has already chosen a preferred supplier before the contract negotiations begin. More often than not, they will award the order to that favorite, but I have seen times when the situation changed during the contract negotiations. Perhaps the company can't accept stipulations in the contract, or the contractual penalties are so harsh that the favorite supplier can't live with them. At this point, the customer is very accommodating toward this favorite candidate. You can feel and see it. Requests for changes to the T&C's are given real consideration, instead of the short "just price it in" answer.

Customers will often go through contract negotiations with two, or even three suppliers, so that more than one candidate is ready to sign on the dotted line. The reasons are multifaceted. As mentioned above, a supplier is more inclined to accept harsh conditions in the contract if they know other bidders are still in the running for an order. Prices are more likely to be negotiated downward for the same reason. Suppliers will be scrambling to give their bottom price offer. And finally, this work can be done parallel to technical negotiations, so after a decision is made the project can start immediately.

When the customer is negotiating with multiple parties, each supplier can develop information or ideas which may have an impact on the final contract. I have been in contract negotiations where the customer suddenly brought up seemingly absurd changes to the contract. This should tell you that they have been discussing the project with someone else, and that someone was able to convince the customer of a feature's value or importance. As far as positioning this could mean three things:

- They really are working with you in mind, and do not want to leave any gaps in the contract. This could be good news.
- They could be testing the idea to see if it really is as big a deal as the other supplier has claimed.
- The customer knows that this new idea is pertinent to that one bidder only, and to force you to use their preferred methods or components will put you at a price disadvantage. It may be a play to convince you to hike your price or lower your profit. In the worst case, it is being used to push you out of the race altogether.

Even though the customer may already have a favorite supplier in mind before contract negotiations begin, it's possible for the situation to quickly change. I have seen this many times, sometimes to my favor and sometimes against me.

> I was discussing a sizeable equipment project with three attorneys from the largest flat box furniture company in the world. One of the sticking points was in the clause of

repair obligation. The contract demanded that if the system didn't work, the supplier would make a first, second, and third attempt to repair it within one week's time. If they were unable to resolve the issue, the customer could hire a third party to repair it at the supplier's cost. I explained to the customer's lawyers that it was not realistic if we would have to design a fix, order parts, install them, try them out, and repeat the process three times (if the first two fixes didn't work) within one week's time when just to order and receive a replacement electrical motor could take anywhere from a couple of days to a few weeks. In the end, they understood my request, and we agreed to a *reasonable expedited repair time*. This was a huge victory from a risk point of view. I was lucky that the attorneys were experienced and actually understood the issue, and were not the kind of folks to just stick to their original demands. (It also told me that I was definitely the front runner at that time.) They just wanted to ensure a working system. We shook hands the next day.

The biggest challenge for a supplier is that rarely are there company representatives on the selling team who completely understand the entire contract as well as the product or project being sold. Because of this, something serious can go wrong. Sometimes a contract is negotiated almost entirely between attorneys. This is fine as far as general language is concerned, but the potential problem with attorney-to-attorney negotiations is that the devil is in the details. Unless the attorney is very familiar with the process or product in the agreement, their input could be limited to percentages, weeks, and obligations.

It is very important that you, as a sales professional, do not bite off more than you can chew. One alternative to prevent this is to pass the contract negotiating part to your manager. You however, should definitely be part of the negotiations because it is your job to learn and understand the contents of the contract. Just be prepared that if someone else hammers out the contract and there are points that are not acceptable to them, the entire sale can disappear in front of your eyes.

> I witnessed the aftermath of an extreme case of contracts while traveling with a government delegation in the Republic of Tatarstan. I met with representatives of a company manufacturing specialty trucks like ambulances, fire trucks, and other specialty vehicles. The vehicles were built on another company's frame and power transmission (a dump truck manufacturer). The representatives told me that their contract with the dump truck manufacturer allowed only the purchase of complete vehicles, including the bucket. They could not buy a truck frame without a dump truck bucket. They had no use for the buckets, so when each dump truck arrived the bucket was stripped off and scrapped. The dump truck manufacturer had a solid contract of their own with a bucket manufacturer, so buying the buckets back from the specialty vehicle maker was out of the question. (The company making the buckets would not benefit from lower demand for their buckets.) Since all buckets were sold for scrap and later melted, perhaps the melted steel was sold back to the original bucket manufacturer?

## Unacceptable Contracts and Bad Contracts: Who Is Responsible?

Larger contracts are a collection of documents produced by different departments. Some are freshly drafted while others have been in use for a long time. One of these documents is often a standardized component list that clearly specifies the preferred parts the customer would like used in the product or service they are buying. The customer may use only components from a particular manufacturer because they want to standardize their spare parts to minimize the inventory they have to keep on hand, or make sure the items are well known to their maintenance department. The components list is reviewed and accepted by the supplier, and then attached to the contract. The same is done with the other specifications that come from the customer.

Each one of these documents is a partial contractual demand from the customer, and a partial contractual promise from the supplier to do exactly what the document states. Therefore, all documents must be completely understood by the seller.

Review everything carefully. It's possible that documentation was not coordinated, and the individual pieces of the contract might not be up to date and consistent. In one document the specification may call for this, and in another the same specification calls for that. Even if the supplier's technical people draft some of the specifications themselves, they have to be very careful choosing the words and numbers they use. This is definitely not the place to overpromise anything, or to write down the performance criteria that the company hopes to achieve. Promises should be played as safely as possible.

The responsibility to put all this together falls on the salesperson. They may not produce all the documents, but they are usually the one putting the package together.

## Defining Contract Details

One of the biggest challenges with contracts I have seen – and there are hundreds of them – is that they lack a clear definition of what is acceptable and what is not. In addition, they are often missing clear steps of how to handle problems when they arise. This is an area where it is worth spending the time to define. If details are clearly defined, it is much easier for both parties to follow the contract.

I created a simple one page form called *Acceptable Performance Criteria*. This form is where we detailed, with a couple dozen lines, exactly when a product was considered to be a completed delivery.

## Decision Making Authority in the Sales Organization

Who decides which contract clauses are acceptable and which are not? There needs to be a clear division of power and responsibilities within the supplier's organization. Every salesperson needs to know how far they can negotiate, and at what point they should pass an issue on to their manager. It seems like a trivial thing, but it is not.

> Pete is a new salesman that works for Company JJJ, which sells and installs fences. Customers can choose from four paint colors. Pete's current customer wants their fence painted a different, non-standard color to match their old fence color. If the customer is willing to supply the paint, should Pete be able to say ok?
>
> There are many aspects to consider. Are the fences painted by Company JJJ, or are they ordered pre painted? Is there a warranty on the paint? The fence supplier uses a particular brand of paint, and has developed a proven method for applying it to their product. The customer's paint will have to be the same quality, and perform at the level of the four standard colors that are supplied. If the paint chips or peels off ten months later, who is responsible? What defines a chip or a peel? What if the color fades?

The real answer of who makes the decision is based on the salesperson's knowledge and experience. The salesperson shouldn't have to ask for a decision about every tiny detail if they know the product and the application. However, if you find yourself in this kind of situation and are unsure of what you should do, pass the question to your manager.

I've dealt with sales managers with no experience, to sales managers with extensive experience. When their decision making power was limited, they, more often than not, expressed their feelings of not being trusted. They often misunderstand why their decision making power is limited. They feel that their boss doesn't trust them when the truth is that all new salespeople need to learn how to approach the sales process, and that takes time. It's actually a good thing for a company to give new salespeople some time to get acclimated before the sales pressure hits them.

Who bears the ultimate responsibility of what is acceptable and what is not? Every salesperson needs someone within their organization that they can rely on if contract negotiations hit a wall. There are times when the salesperson either accepts the customer's requirements and hopes for the best, or walks away. This is a tough call to make, especially when the customer's representative is sitting across the table telling the salesperson, "You are the only one with a problem with this. Are you sure you are not overreacting?" Under these conditions, most people end up signing and hoping for the best because the consequences of walking away can be monetized immediately in the form of a lost sale whereas problems in the contract appear only later.

> I was at a final purchase meeting at a customer's site in Germany. I was the only supplier present, and the customer had indicated they wanted to iron out a contract with us that day. The final price had already been agreed in advance. I was sitting at the table with our German territory representative. The customer had three representatives sitting across from us, including a

corporate attorney. I was handed the contract for the first time.

It was basically all good except for *one little thing*. I noticed a stipulation that stated if any part of the large system must be repaired or replaced during the 12 month warranty period, a new 12 month warranty for the entire system, and all of its components, would start again from that repair or replacement date.

I told the customer that I couldn't sign something like that, and explained that according to industry practice the new repaired/replacement part would get a new warranty, but not the entire system. With a value of €3.5 million, there were so many components that something could easily break down. Our company did not make the standard electrical, mechanical, or automation components. We built the equipment from purchased parts. I also pointed out that some of the components manufacturers only gave us a 12 month warranty from their ship date, which could be 6-8 months prior to our start-up, so we were already taking a risk.

The customer told me that every one of their suppliers had signed their T&C's, with no exceptions. "If you do not sign it as is, please excuse yourself from the discussions, and we will invite bidder #2 to come in and we will place the order with them." They added that they had never enforced that particular clause with any of their suppliers, but it was there for their security if "a supplier started being difficult." I told them I was sorry, but if they were unable or unwilling to change the clause, I would have to walk away. The response was, "Have a safe drive to the airport."

After showing my manager the contract he responded, "Well, if they said they would not use the clause, why didn't you just sign?" I was floored. I had really expected the president of the company to praise me for not sticking the company's neck out. Knowing all this, what would you have done?

If I did sign this contract, everything could have gone well. But, if I signed it and everything went badly, who would have been at fault? Would I have lost my job for giving away a never ending warranty on €3.5 million worth of equipment? This is why responsibility must be so clear that everyone understands the potential ramifications, both good and bad. Also, the decision maker supporting the salesperson must be available to give advice at the time of the negotiations, not a couple days or weeks after.

## A Project Gone Bad: Pointing Fingers

If a contract was signed even if it looked and felt unacceptable, and something happened during delivery that drove the cost higher than anticipated at the time of the sale, now what? Who's at fault?

This can transpire weeks, months, or even years after a contract was signed and the project was started. Over the years, I have seen that out of every ten projects about six or seven go exactly as planned, one to two go slightly better than planned and then there seems to always be the one that ends up a total financial catastrophe. These bad projects eat into the profits from the good projects.

Again, no one expected at the time of the sale that it would turn into a bad project. If you can include enough money in the price for the unknown to occur, it may end up being a good project or even better than average, but who's to decide what amount of money is enough? Plus, at some point after adding enough cost, you will lose the order to another competitor because of price. So, the entire exercise is moot. It is by far more beneficial for the company to not enter into a clearly risky project in the first place than to enter into one only to find out 6-20 months later that the project was a disaster.

Even if you use help to make decisions during contract negotiations, please be aware that afterwards most of the blame for those bad projects ends up with sales. That means you. According to engineering, production, or field services it was sold wrong. One way to mitigate this problem is to get all the departments involved during the quotation phase, so everyone has a chance to voice their opinion and comment *prior* to the sale closing.

# 19.

# RULES AND ETHICS OF SELLING

*Caveat emptor* is a very old Latin phrase, which means "Let the buyer beware." We all are taught from early on to behave morally and treat others like we would like to be treated. They are noble words to live by, but do they translate to work? What about in sales? I believe they should. So, why has there been an age-old phrase warning us about the dangers of buying?

Other teachings center on taking the high road; doing what's morally and ethically right. But what if you had to choose between doing the right thing and making enough money to feed your family? The perceived answer is not so clear anymore. People may start telling little *white lies*. What is a white lie? White refers to pure, or clean. Lie, on the other hand, is dirty and negative. By attaching the prefix of white to a negative and dirty word we justify lying; we make it less severe and almost acceptable. Our intentions are good. After all, it's really not that big a lie, or a lie at all. It's more an omission, or better yet, "It is my opinion." On the scale of lies, is there anything more innocent than a little white lie?

> Kenny sells new cars and his cars have a warranty of 50,000 miles. What if a customer asks if it is the best warranty offered by anyone? Does he say yes or does he say no, someone else gives a better one? Hmm, he thinks. Define *best*. He, as a salesperson, can justify his answer by choosing the interpretation that best suits him. If he believes that his warranty is the best available, he most likely can answer, "Absolutely not, ours is the best

one." If the same customer asks, "Does anyone offer a warranty with higher mileage than your 50,000 miles?" Now, he is in the red zone. He knows for a fact that there are companies in the industry advertising warranties up to 100,000 miles. So, how does he answer? He answers by diverting attention away from the direct answer. He says, "Well, there are companies advertising lengthier warranties based on mileage, but they don't come close to matching the quality of our warranty."

So back we go to *caveat emptor*. In the end, it is the customer who carries the ultimate responsibility to ask the right questions. This is one of the reasons why successful salespeople are excellent buyers. They know the techniques used by salespeople, and can ask the right questions.

Choices become more difficult for the salesperson when the morally or ethically right answer puts the success of a sale at risk. I am by no means implying that salespeople struggle with these choices; I am outright claiming they do. Again, the justification for even thinking this way has always been that it is up to the buyer to ask the right questions. It is not anyone's duty to disclose all the possible flaws of their product when competitors are not doing it. This issue is society wide where marketing always stresses product strengths and good points, or throwing mud on the competitor. Look at political campaigns!

I am not saying that you should ditch your high morals and values. I am saying that the real world quickly teaches its customs to the bright eyed sales student. It can be a tough lesson to learn that, unfortunately, sales is one of the professions where it is possible for some people to advance by stomping on others, being shrewd, and only telling half truths. In order to survive in this industry, you have to be aware that it does happen.

There is a lot of talk around the general ethics and rules of selling. What exactly, are these rules? Who sets them up? Who enforces them?

There are no real rules on how to sell, per se, but there are laws. There are consumer protection laws, product safety standards, and thousands of other rules and regulations that a product is governed by. And, of course, they vary from one country to another. Regardless of what and where you sell, there are some that apply to you, your methods, and your product. Make sure you talk to your manager and find out which ones pertain to your job and your product. Make sure you know what you can and can't do or say – especially when you are dealing with a contract. A common misperception is that as long as you don't break any general laws, you're all set. Easy, right? Not so fast.

When dealing in international business, a salesperson quickly finds that the rules are not executed in the same manner around the world. In some places, it is expected that the salesperson brings a gift for each of the customer decision makers: perhaps a lighter or a cell phone. Bribes are commonplace within certain cultures, or are not enforced as vigorously in every country.

This is one of the reasons many companies have incorporated buying teams for large purchasing decisions, as discussed earlier, to offset and eliminate any chances of unethical behavior. The team is big enough and diverse enough so that no bidder can even think of making a shady deal with every member. This ensures solid reasoning is used in making a decision for or against suppliers.

It is a bumpy winding road of morals and ethics for the salesperson. If you disagree and think the issue is black and white, consider the following questions:

- Is it ethical to compare one product to another one?
- Is it ethical to compare only the one feature that is better in product A than it is in product B in order to sell it?

- Is it ethical to tell a potential customer that you have heard that the other company is about to go out of business because of lack of funding?
- Is it ok to flaunt your opinions as facts?
- Is it ok to make up statistics as you go?
- How much responsibility do you put on the customer to find out information on their own?
- Do you only praise your own product, or do you also throw mud at the competitor's product and company?

These all are decisions that you must make. Over the years, I have met salespeople who took pride in themselves and their product, and often announced upfront that they would not talk badly of any competitors and would only speak highly of their own product. Then, I have seen the salesperson that did nothing but throw mud on the competition. I have also seen both styles successfully win an order too. It depends on the customer.

Most companies post their ethics and morals on their website: nice words strung together into statements of how the company likes to be viewed. However, the true picture is revealed in how their salespeople behave. If it seems a company or individual is acting unethically in their sales process, the only one who can do anything about it is the customer. If the customer does not like the unethical behavior, they have the power to stop it. They can buy from someone else.

Always remember that your style and the kind of salesperson you want to be is your choice.

Thank you, and good luck!

# BIBLIOGRAPHY

Bureau of Labor Statistics, U.S. Department of Labor, *Occupational Employment and Wages*, May 2014, 41-4011, "Sales Representatives, Wholesale and Manufacturing, Technical and Scientific Products"

Bureau of Labor Statistics, U.S. Department of Labor, *Occupational Outlook Handbook*, 2014-2015, "Top Executives," http://www.bls.gov/ooh/management/top-executives.htm

Bureau of Labor Statistics, U.S. Department of Labor, *The Economics Daily*, "Time Spent in Leisure Activities in 2014 by Gender, Age, and Educational Attainment," http://www.bls.gov/opub/ted/2015/time-spent-in-leisure-activities-in-2014-by-gender-age-and-educational-attainment.htm

Berger, Jonah, *Contagious Why Things Catch On*, Simon & Schuster (2013)

Boone & Kurtz, *Contemporary Marketing, Marketing Plan*, Cencage Learning (2011)

Cichelli, David J., *World at Work*, "2012 Sales Compensation Trends Survey Results", January 6, 2012

Iverson, Ken and Varian, Tom, *Plain Talk, Lessons From a Business Maverick*, John Wiley & Sons, Inc, (1998)

Martin, Steve W. "Seven Personality Traits of Top Salespeople", *Harvard Business Review*, June 27, 2011

Meister, Jeanne, "Job Hopping Is the 'New Normal' for Millenials: Three Ways to Prevent a Human Resource Nightmare", *Forbes*, August 14, 2012

Rumbauskas, Frank J. Jr., *Never Cold Call Again*, Wiley (2006)

*Selling Power*, "2014 Sales Training Companies Top Twenty Listing,"Visited June 20, 2015

Skonnard, Aaron, "Why Sales Commissions Don't Work (in the Long Run)," *Inc. Magazine*, August 12, 2014

Stoeckmann, Jim, *World at Work*, "2012 Quota Practices Study," December 19, 2012

Monga, Vipal and Chasan, Emily, "The 109,894-Word Annual Report: As Regulators Require More Disclosures, 10-Ks Reach Epic Lengths; How Much is Too Much?," *The Wall Street Journal*, June 01, 2015